Haipin
The Student's Wife

☐ *A common immigrant*
☐ *A hardworking citizen*

Haipin & family
Kansas U 5/22/1978

By Dr. Richard T. Li

Fort Worth, Texas, USA
2005

© **2005** By Richard T. Li. All rights reserved
Printed by Great Impressions, 434 West Mockingbird
Dallas, Texas 75247 USA, (214) 631-2665
Library of Congress Control Number: **2005902798**
ISBN 0-9675988-5-0
Cover design by: Chris Ollier
Editing by Clara B. Tarver

This book is available online at major booksellers in the
United States
For more information contact:
Fax: 817.656.4138
Email: w007745@airmail.net
Website: http://web2.airmail.net/w007745

The Preface

The American Dream

Every year thousands of immigrants come to the United States, many become permanent residents, and many become American citizens. Though each immigrant differs in interests to be pursued in the great land of opportunities, everyone shares a common goal; that is, to have a successful career that would fully develop the individual's potential without political, religious, or other discrimination boundaries. The United States' basic value of freedom of choice and justice for all provides such a wonderful land that people can make their dreams become true.

'American Dream' should not be referred as only for those who are millionaires, billionaires, Nobel Prize winners, or members of a hall of fame. American dream could be achieved by anyone, such as the key character of Haipin in this book.

Haipin*, the Student's Wife is a true story of a hardworking immigrant woman who starts her adult life as a schoolteacher, but slowly transforms into a workaholic, a devoted student wife, and a lovely mother in the Promised Land. As a child, Haipin was the spoiled daughter of a successful businessman in Manila, but she threw away her privileged background to marry a poor soldier working his way through college in Taiwan. Then, as an F2 student spouse visa holder, she

3

supported her husband financially while he worked through college in the United States. She turned no job offer down, seeing them all as valuable opportunities. For her tireless efforts, every employer she ever worked for awarded her with countless accolades. With her hard work, love, and understanding, this amazing woman helped her husband earn college degrees and secure his career in teaching and administration, as well as guide her children to success. The story of Haipin is another kind of American Dream--a strong family bound by ties of love and understanding.

The author is proud to present this book to Haipin as a gift of love and congratulations on her 40th anniversary, October 25, 2004.

Haipin is a pen name and Yan Yun is that of her husband's. The couple had an interest in writing and publishing during their college years.

ABOUT THE AUTHOR

Richard T. Li, was born in a remote rural mountain village, Yuan Bei, Quidong County, at the southeast corner of Hunan Province in China. His childhood and early adult years were spent living within the destruction of the Japanese invasion of China during World War II and the subsequent Chinese Civil War between the Nationalist government and the Communists' Liberation Army. He came to the United States from Taiwan in 1967 and became an American citizen in 1977. He earned four college degrees, three from American higher education institutions. Li's career in education in the United States included positions as public school teacher, junior college library assistant director, and university professor. He retired from his career in education in 1997. His biographical profile has been included in Marquis Who's Who in America, since 57th Edition, 2003. Li lives in Fort Worth, Texas with wife, Felisa (*pen name Haipin*).

Table Of Contents

ONE

The Island Paradise

Chapter One

The Happy Girl

Haipin, as a child, never spent a day in a bad mood; she was always happy, enjoying life on the island paradise. Her memory could go back to her very early childhood.

Her parents were busy with their business, the TCP Shipping Agency. With the help of eight maids and the same number of male servants, in assisting business and family chores, the kids really enjoyed their daily life with fewer parents' assignments and restrictions. These spoiled kids usually engaged in street activity with neighbor children. They might do things that would not help them develop good skills for adult life. For example, brothers Louis, Andreas, Bicente, Talinto and sister, Maria might work at the family shipping business for a while, then hang out with neighbor kids the rest of the day.

Quite different from her siblings, Haipin's interests were reading, visiting the beach, going to parties with close friends and classmates. She was less interested in traditional home skills for girls, such as cooking, quilting and knitting, as was commonly observed in the Chinese community in the Philippines.

Reading and writing were Haipin's favorite subjects in school. She ranked as the top student in her reading class for the number of books she read from the teacher's reading list. Frequently she was chosen to present a book report to the class orally.

Interest in reading usually motivates people to writing. Haipin had benefited from her reading habit. Her contributing articles were printed in the school paper, magazines, and the local Chinese language newspapers.

At that time, printed material was very expensive to produce. In order to motivate a student's interest in writing, almost all schools, public or private, large or small, secondary, colleges, or universities, would sponsor the most common economic publication, the Wall News Bulletin, known as Wall Paper, and post it on the wall. It could be a monthly or bi-monthly publication. The printed edition of the newsletter could be a semester project. Features on a Wall Paper covered local news, national news, world news, school activity news, editor's page, cartoons, jokes, short essays, poems, etc. Haipin liked contributing articles to the paper, sharing what she read, whether fiction or romance stories. Most of her magazine and newspaper articles were written during her college years.

Haipin has kept her interest in reading and writing from her young school years to college and adult life as well. She had her own library at home. Romance stories were her favorite reading and thus became her personal library's main collection. The next category was motion picture magazines. She would be able to tell the profile of popular movie stars both in Chinese and American motion pictures. She started writing in a diary in the sixth grade. Nothing was more devastating to her than when a fire burned her family home and destroyed her private library collection.

The academic oriented girl was in no way a bookworm. Haipin was active in extracurricular also. She would not miss any school sponsored services for either the local Filipino or Chinese communities. The Chinese immigrants traditionally are very conservative and maintain their culture. Haipin, though a young girl, would enthusiastically participate in the community's celebration of Chinese festivals, such as Chinese Lunar New Year, Autumn Festival, etc.

Enjoying Nature's Environment

The islands' country, the Philippines, with tropical weather, indeed could be called a paradise. People wear short sleeve shirts year round. Manila, the capital city, has many good seashore beaches as well as scenic mountains. Visitors from foreign countries who live in a high altitude of the Northern Hemisphere would be surprised to see mango and papaya parks, as opposed to the forest with evergreen pine trees, with which the tourists were more familiar. As a Manila resident, Haipin enjoyed wonderful times at these resort areas.

In a tropical environment, people consider the beach as a major recreation resort. Kids liked the idea too. As a country of many islands, the Philippines has many beaches also. The residents in metropolitan Manila certainly enjoyed their leisure time strolling along the beaches.

Haipin was one of many kids that enjoyed nature and the beauty of the sea. She would like to see the vast water, the waves, the surfing boats, and the sea gulls. On holidays or weekends she might invite close friends to take a walk on the nearby seashore, singing her favorite songs, sharing her feelings and dreams with friends. On each trip Haipin would pick out a piece of seashell or rock as a souvenir for that visit.

Besides water and seashores, Manila has a place known as a scenic resort called Baguio, which is a resort attraction in the mountains that is high enough to have non-tropical plants, which attract tourists and serves as a retreat for people locally, as well as around the world. It is another attraction that Haipin would like to visit for an out of city refreshing trip. She began to visit there during her early elementary school years.

Another point of interest for the happy girl to visit was Davao City. After her sister Maria married and settled down in that city, Haipin could not consider any more exciting summer vacation than frequently visiting the island resort, Davao City which happened to be her sister's residence. Davao City is located in the southern most part the Philippines. It is located at about four degrees north of the equator. The weather is very warm year around. A large papaya park was within a short walking distance from her sister's house. Haipin liked to play with neighbor kids there. Occasionally she would visit the nearby mango garden for a picnic. The sweet, tasty mango became visitors' nature dessert, fresh from the mango tree.

The tourists would not miss a point of interest known as the 'Pearl Factory Island'. The PFI belongs to the island Sarangani group. It would take the visitor about one hour to travel by boat to land on the island. Haipin toured there several times. First, she was curious about the process of culturing pearls that would become precious jewelry. After getting bored, she would play at the seashore beach; playing water games, or sailing around the island, then taking a break on the different beaches singing and dancing on the sands.

The Mixture of Cultures and Languages

Though Chinese is a minority in the Philippines, the capital, which is Manila, has a large Chinese ethnic community. Of the hard working immigrants, some of them are successful businessmen, but the majority of the Chinese immigrants are financially sound. Most native Filipino would not discriminate or reject Chinese culture. They welcomed such rich civilization and diligent immigrants making contributions to their society. Although Haipin went to a Chinese school, she got along well, both with classmates in her Chinese school and the local kids as well. She can speak her parents' native dialect, the Filipino Tagalot, the Chinese mandarin, English, and Spanish.

Haipin's parents came from the Chinese coastal province of Fujian in the early 1920s. China had long time warlords and poverty during the Chin Dynasty. The 1911 revolution would not be able to turn the economy around in a short time. People in the Chinese mainland still considered overseas as a Promised Land to find a better life. Emigration to foreign countries was a hot pursuance for many people who lived in coastal provinces such as Fujian and Guangdong.

The majority of emigrants from Fujian preferred the Philippines, while emigrants from Guangdon Province chose Thailand and Indonesia as their favorite adopted homeland. Financially the Chinese did not bring big capital to the Philippines, however, most of them became successful businessmen through hard work, thus making important contributions to the local economy.

Haipin could not understand how her father could pay for eight maids to take care of home chores (taking care of kids, laundry, cooking) and the same number of male helpers for helping with the shipping business. The young girl did enjoy immediate attention by people around the house. Her parents were so busy running the family business, they could hardly find time to spend with Haipin. Her father, in his mid 50s, spoiled her as much as he could. Dad never declined to fulfill Haipin's wish lists. However, her mother who was much younger than her husband, played a little tougher role in disciplining Haipin.

Despite her father's lack of formal education, he always praised Haipin for her interest in school. On the contrary, her mother, also without formal education, had little concern for her kids' education. Haipin's siblings would like, instead, to stay home doing family errands, than go to school. Her mother was pleased with the kids who spent less time on schoolwork so they could spend more time around her. In fact, the number of maids and male helpers was enough to run errands. Haipin's sisters and brothers actually spent their time on their own interests such as sports, gambling, personal relationships with peer boys and girls. They married as young as age 15.

Haipin was a mid-class family kid and could be enjoying things that kids liked at that age within the social environment of that time. However, she pursued interests in different directions than her siblings and neighbor kids. Instead of searching for fun in city streets as most kids did, Haipin was active at school sponsored activities on and off campus. On weekends or holidays, she would spend the entire day with peer friends on the resort beaches and mountains.

Though a young city girl with an abundance of her father's trust and support, the spoiled Haipin never became addicted to luxury, material things and out of control behavior. She liked school. She was interested in reading. She kept a diary as a part of her daily chore.

The outdoor activities: the beach, the mountain trail, and social life, helped the little girl develop a good interpersonal personality with a wide spectrum to see the world. In addition to her classmates and neighborhood kids, she reached out to overseas pen pal relationships. Since she attended Chinese language school in Manila, Haipin subscribed to Chinese magazines published in Taiwan and Hong Kong. And from the personal section she encountered and kept pen pal friends.

As a popular student, Haipin was frequently chosen as a student representative to welcome school visitors. At a time, 1950-60s, when the Republic of China (Taiwan) and the Republic of the Philippines maintained a normal diplomatic relationship, the Chinese (Taiwan) naval ships occasionally visited the Philippines as goodwill missions to strengthen friendship between the two countries. Chinese schools in the Philippines would select student representatives to welcome the ships, sailors, and naval officers. Haipin was very interested in playing a role of 'welcome angel' for the visiting naval officers from her parents' motherland. Her popularity and willingness to help others always made her win the assignment easily.

Haipin's academic major was teaching at the Chiang Kai-shek College. She prepared for a career to work with elementary kids in the Chinese community. Her college education helped her build a strong base in bicultural and bilingual: the Filipino and the Chinese.

Admiring China's long, rich cultural history, her mind focused more on the Chinese. She enjoyed reading Chinese fiction and watching Chinese movies.

Devoting her career to teaching, Haipin worked with the elementary kids, since she earned a teaching degree from college. It was an unfortunate situation that government laws placed tough restrictions on Chinese school operations. The funding of private schools in the Chinese community was not very stable. A teacher's contract was not a term legal paper, but rather worked as a note of intention. However, it did not bother the young teacher. Haipin worked, not for how much she earned, but for how much she enjoyed teaching the kids in her class. In case her school was closed for a while, Haipin would look for a tutoring opportunity. Should a substituting position become available, she would seek this job without considering the cost of transportation. This is the nature of a mid-class family kid, Haipin, who had a big heart for school children.

Open Mind on Overseas

As romance emerged in her personal life, Haipin, the young schoolteacher had her mind set on widening horizons in searching for her dream one. Though her mom had her mind on looking for a local male for her, Haipin sought friends beyond local boundaries. She had an open mind that was not a normal practice at that time, especially in the very conservative Chinese community. Haipin kept up communication with several pen pals; all of whom lived overseas. She had several young Chinese (Taiwan) naval officer friends that she got to know while their ships were visiting Manila. With this kind of social orientation, Haipin had widened her horizons in picking out her man. However, by the overwhelmingly good impression these young military officers gave, she could not turn away from noticing their strong muscles, good looks and good manners. The officers had bombarded the young girl with romantic letters, gifts, and telegrams. Haipin, thus, was no longer interested in mom's advice to look for love locally. In similar pursuance, her close female high school classmates moved in the same direction. They studied and earned academic degrees at universities in Taiwan. Since their naval officer boy friends were around for taking care of them, Haipin was a little jealous of their campus life and social activity in their parents' motherland.

However, the happy girl had a good reason to maintain her optimism on finding a dream military officer overseas. Her long-time pen pal, Yan-Yun , a young Army Captain, had just been discharged from military service. He was now a college student, working on a Bachelor's degree at a university in Taipei, the capital of the Republic of China (Taiwan). She began to respond to his mail during her senior year in high school. The marathon style pen pal relationship had been on and off for six years. Despite the absence of personal contact, romantic correspondence made the two remote pen pal lovers feel just as sweet and as close as if she were in his warm arms.

Haipin believed she could choose her own future; education, career, and marriage without difficulty. Dad was always at her side. Mom's opposition could be softening, should Haipin change to a more reasonable and less firm stand on the choice of her destiny.

Unfortunately Haipin lost a big supporter. Her father passed away at a critical time when she had to choose a college and start social activities with boys. It gave the young girl reason for a tough fight against her mother's will.

The mother tried hard to convince Haipin that she stood firmly on her personal life; specifically on dating and marriage. Mother wanted Haipin to know that her being tough on her was for her happiness. Any responsible and caring mother she believed must take a tough stand in order to protect a young daughter from falling into a love temptation pitfall. Mother opposed pen pal relationships. She did not believe the honor and truthfulness of the person she did not have a chance to talk to in person. Neither did she want Haipin marrying a military man. The worse thing she could imagine was if the man lived overseas. She would not be able to know her daughter's family life, or if Haipin was being abused.

Therefore, mother's tactics for stopping Haipin's intention to look for love and marriage overseas were twofold. One was financially rewarding. Mom promised to transfer a large amount of her family's liquid assets to her, should she start a family in the local community. Another one was to throw a scare into her daughter, making her believe that physical violent abuse could not be avoided when marrying a soldier.

However, the smart young girl had her defense strategy too. Haipin avoided having head-on clashes with her mom. In a subtle way she told her mother that her priority was placed on a right guy in the local community. However, she would consider the personal quality of the guy over geographic location. The argument over Haipin's own choice of a boy friend and one chosen by her mother had created a strain between mother and daughter. As time went by, the mom softened her stand on her daughter's love and marriage; Haipin won her adult rights to choose her boy friend.

In the spring of 1964, there was no seasonal change in Manila. Haipin, then an elementary school teacher, received an unusual amount of air mail, one letter a week, from her pen pal, Yan Yun, a young army Captain, turned college student in Taipei, Taiwan. Though Yan Yun was in his college senior year with tremendous pressure on preparation for graduation and trying to secure a job after earning a Bachelor's degree, he still spent time writing to Haipin. He simply could not stop thinking of the sweet young woman in his daily life. Spring is still chilly in northern Taipei. However, his mind was lingering on escorting Haipin in and out of movie houses, restaurants, beaches and parks in warm Manila. April is the time when schools are on a semester break in the Philippines. Haipin spent some of her vacation time at her sister's home in southern Philippines.

Coincidentally, students in Taiwan would enjoy a week-long spring break in March or April. Meanwhile, Yan Yun took a couple of days of his spring break to tour southern Taiwan. The tropical climate in southern Taiwan is also warm most of the year. The tall cocoa trees lined river shores and city streets of Kao Hsiung, a major harbor city in southern Taiwan, creating a vivid scenic picture of Haipin's vacation resort on islands of the southern Philippines. Yan Yun wished he could share a happy vacation with Haipin, either in Taiwan or the Philippines. At this moment, looking at the horizon of the sea, Yan Yun wished that one of the sea gulls could bring his greeting to the girl across the strait. As he returned to college from spring break, he decided to give Haipin a big surprise.

Despite Maria's strong desire for her sister to stay with her longer, Haipin expressed eagerly her intention to go home. She missed very much reading Yan Yun's mail. When she got home from a three-week vacation, mail and magazines were piled up on her desk. First, she picked up the airmailed ones from Taipei. The familiar envelope, designed with familiar handwriting caught her attention most. Among Yan Yun's mail, one letter was unusually thin. This one worried her, because it broke his routine of three pages or more. Haipin thought it might be his final message, ending the pen pal relationship. To keep from avoiding possible disappointment, she read the other mail before opening the thin one. Every piece of Yan Yun's mail was passionate and expressed how he missed her. Then she opened the thin mail with her heart pounding with uncertainty.

Dear H,

*I love you. Please accept my engagement proposal. Sign and return to me the legal form when you receive the document from separate mail. Be **a student wife** for a short time, I still have one semester to go for my Bachelor's degree. Love, YY*

It was a total surprise to the skeptical, yet optimistic young woman. For quite a while Haipin thought that something, either better or worse, would end the friendship while their correspondence continued into the sixth year. Haipin had dreamed of getting good news for some time, so the engagement proposal was indeed a happy ending.

She considered Yan Yun's proposal seriously. On the positive side, she admired his determination to prepare for a bright future by continuing to improve himself in the challenging world of education and career. Yan Yun was a young solder who fought in the Chinese Civil War in the late 1940s and early 1950s. After losing the war to the Chinese Communists, his unit retreated to Taiwan. At age 25 he was promoted to the rank of Army Captain. At 30, he left the Army and was admitted to a civilian college to study for a Bachelor's degree. During the six years of correspondence they exchanged family background, sharing personal interests and dreams. The feeling of being so close, yet still so remote could be found in volumes of albums with numerous pictures: personal, social activities, vacations. She felt it was the right time to say 'yes'.

From another point of view, Haipin might consider the uncertainty or nightmare of marrying a man without understanding him in person. A personal quality could only be revealed by personal social contact. She did not have this kind of close observation on his behavior and attitudes toward women. What if he was crazy with a bad temper, or a male dominant believer? Could anyone believe all those love letters without any doubt? Haipin never had questions on his honesty during the years' of correspondence of sharing thoughts and dreams. Even now she still trusted him. At this moment she must take this under strong consideration.

The strong force that kept her from accepting Yan Yun's proposal came form her mom. Mother considered her daughter's choice as the worst foolish action possible. First, mother urged Haipin's siblings to persuade their sister to turn down Yan Yun's proposal. Indeed, for a family's closeness reasons, they would like Haipin not to seek love overseas. However, her siblings loved her and respected her decision. Since Haipin was the only college educated one in the family, the sisters and brothers were very proud of their sister's academic accomplishment, and thus were reluctant to take any action against her will. On the contrary, the siblings pleaded with mother to change her mind, believing that Haipin was a smart girl with a college education. She had the ability to make a good decision. For her happiness, mother should not disappoint Haipin. Siblings thus reversed their efforts, working hard in order to soften mother's opposition.

Disappointed in not making a decision for her daughter's marriage, mother took an indifferent position with a non-involvement attitude. Haipin, then, got needed support from her siblings. Her elder brother, Louis, acted for her Mother's legal position and signed the engagement paper.

Haipin was aware that her victory over mom's opposition hurt her mother's feelings. Thinking of her widowed, loving mother, Haipin felt guilty for her disobedient behavior as a selfish daughter. The emotional turmoil was strong. She was happy for her dream coming true, but sorry for missing her beloved mom and siblings in the near future.

The happy girl faced the most difficult decision in her life. It took Haipin a couple of weeks of thinking about the consequence of her decision. Seemingly the odds against her were so strong. She quietly made a visitation to her father's tomb, praying:

"Dad, You always gave me good advice when I needed help. I am facing a dilemma, either accepting or declining Yan Yun's engagement proposal. Though you remain silent, I'll have peace of mind when I make this important decision. This visit will help me get out of a dilemma and make a wise choice."

Upon returning home from visiting her father's tomb, Haipin invited Louis to have lunch at a restaurant. She told her brother of her graveside visit to their father's tomb and indicated favor to accept Yan Yun's proposal. Louis was more than happy to help his sister in anyway. Being an elder son of the family, Louis substituted for his reluctant mom and put his signature on the engagement legal form as evidence of parent's approval.

Haipin wrote a letter of acceptance to Yan Yun's proposal. In a sense of treating a serious legal document, she placed the mail on hold for a couple of weeks. She had already solicited advice from her classmates who were either married to naval officers in Taiwan or attended universities in Taipei. This time she reviewed evaluations of Yan Yun from those who had a chance to meet him in person. Her classmates provided her with Yan Yun's looks, personality, strengths and weaknesses.

She then mailed the letter of acceptance with the engagement paper on a lucky day for engagement and marriage, chosen from the Chinese farmers' calendar (lunar year calendar).

Yan Yun did not take a long time to respond. Within a week he suggested that Haipin set a wedding date, either in the summer, immediately after spring semester, or during the fall semester before his gradation from college. Thus, the happy girl was busy preparing for her new life as a student wife.

TWO

The Quarter Part of a Chicken

Chapter Two

Love Adventure

With great expectation and uncertainty Haipin began preparing a journey of adventure to a dream world that, for better or worse, would change her life. The six year long pen-pal relationship was just about to end, facing the reality of possible adversity. However, at that moment, Haipin had only one thing on her mind, and that was to meet the man who had been in her dream life for so long.

The final decision came. Haipin sent by registered airmail the signed engagement paper with messages of her sincere blessing for a happy family life ahead. It was on a day marked as 'good for engagement and wedding' in the farmer's almanac calendar. She did everything she could to assure there would be good luck.

By surprise, in two days Haipin got Yan Yun's confirmation by special delivery mail, which was the fastest postal service in Taiwan in the 1960s. Even more astonishing to her was his plan to set the wedding in Taipei in October, right after his mid-term exams in college. For an early start of the preparation of the wedding ceremony, he invited her to come to Taiwan in the coming summer. Haipin was aware that Yan Yun did not have relatives in Taiwan, because communication with his family in the China mainland was totally cut off after the Communists' victory. Yan Yun was sort of a helpless, poor student. Hopefully, Haipin believed that she could help him reduce some stress caused by academic work and part-time employment. She thus answered Yan Yun with a positive 'yes'.

Haipin then wasted no time; she contacted a travel agency for legal papers (Visa, health certificate), airline flight schedule and foreign currency. This time she did not want to think whether or not she could get along well with Yan Yun. Everything in her mind was love for the young veteran army captain and college senior, and a hope for happiness for the couple's future. Haipin was excited over the independence of her life. Her mother never believed her daughter's choice would work. She would not pay much attention to Haipin because of her daughter's disobedience concerning her advice. The Chinese Civil War made Yan Yun cut off contact with his parents. He did not have any family authority to advise him on this matter.

The feeling of a big family event was difficult, with the absence of parental greetings and wishes, which was unfortunate. Haipin thought of it in a different way. Her new life in Taiwan would be free from unwanted calls or visits by in-laws. Another advantage of her living in the tropic island of Taiwan was that she could speak fluent Mandarin, the official national language of the Republic of China; she could also speak the local Taiwanese dialect.

When summer comes to Taiwan, people living in the north of the island feel some degree warmer than the folks residing in the tropic south. All schools are in summer sessions. Yan Yun did not enroll in the college summer programs. Instead, he worked full time for a government street-widening project in the capital city. He needed additional income to pay for the wedding. His big project and great expectation now was to meet Haipin for the first time and prepare for the upcoming wedding banquet.

Haipin had been working on the Taiwan visit quietly since she accepted the engagement proposal and the tentative travel schedule. It would break her mother's heart if she knew Haipin was preparing to leave home for Taipei. Haipin therefore, treated this project in a very low profile manner, feeling that her mother would not detect any suspicious behavior. Haipin believed as long as she did not openly challenge her mom's authority that she would ignore the whole thing.

Among her family members, only her brother Louis, her strong supporter, knew details about Haipin's plans. Louis promised his sister that he would not let mother know when the flight would depart from Manila to Taipei.

Outside her home, Hapin got a lot of help from friends. One of her best friends, a former classmate, provided a temporary haven to protect her secrecy. Haipin removed her favorite personal belongings one by one, from her families' home to the classmate's home.

She would stop at the friend's home, bringing new purchases made at the shopping mall, mostly designer clothes or jewelry. Therefore, the readiness for travel was made easier.

The day before her flight departure to Taipei, Haipin visited her father's tomb praying for blessings from her beloved father. Then, she brought good food home to her mom. For some reason her mother did not say anything, and did not seem to enjoy the food. Instead, she gave the plate to the maid who prepared daily lunch for Haipin during her school years.

The departure day came. Most family members thought it was just a normal day for the Tan's young girl. Haipin kept cool, showing no unusual emotion. She did tell her mom that she would leave home shortly for a social activity. One of her friends was leaving for the United States. Mother's answer was predictable; 'have fun.'

However, deep in her heart, Haipin felt guilty for not being able to reveal her true story to her mother. In this world, a mother is the most trusted woman in a daughter's life, and Haipin failed to honor the trust. 'Should my father still be alive, he would escort me to the airport and all family members would happily join him to pray for my good luck.' Hapin could not help but think back to her childhood of her daddy's love and care. Now she was about to change her life forever. There was no greeting from either of her parents on such a big occasion. Haipin wished everything would go well.

Haipin tried hard to keep from shedding tears as she left home for the airport. No one in the family, her brothers, sister, maids, or business employees had ever noticed her unusual day of activity. She was lucky that no emergency arose that would call for her to stay and ruin her travel schedule.

As she got out of the bus at the airport, her friends waved hands welcoming her. Haipin was very impressed by their help. Luggage was already put in line for check in. It came to Haipin's mind that in some cases good friends could help her better than her family members. Upon completing boarding procedures, Haipin spent a few minutes chatting with friends. Everyone wished her a safe trip and good luck for her new life in Taiwan. She regretted that none of her dear family members were there for her departure.

It was less than two hours flight time from Manila to Taipei. Haipin sat by the window. This was her first overseas travel. She had mixed feelings. As Manila disappeared from view she couldn't help but feel a longing for her childhood, her school, and all the familiar places in the capital city.

"How long might it be before I see my folks? Or, in the worse situation, mother would never understand me. I might be in a love exile in a foreign land until her passing away." Then she continued to imagine.

"Why should I worry? Yan Yun loves me. We have
been good pen-pal friends for six years.   Now we
are planning to marry. Although we miss our
parents' care, we will feel our life is more free."

Her feeling of mixed emotion was interrupted by the
Captain's announcement of landing preparation.

Looking out the window as the plane approached the
city, Haipin could not believe her eyes.

"Is it Taipei? Why did the airline send me back
to Manila on the same flight? "

The similarity of landscaping features between the
two cities surprised Haipin. Hills surround Taipei. One
can see the large water area of Taiwan Strait in the east
of the island and the Pacific Ocean to the west. Manila
Bay is located in the major island of Luzon, with the
Pacific Ocean to the east and the South China Sea to the
west. It gave Haipin the first impression of not being a
total stranger where geographical environment is
concerned.

In the 1960s Taiwan was an under developed, poor
country. The nation's economy was no better than that
of the Philippines. Haipin did not pay much attention to
the facilities of the Taipei International Airport,
compared to the Manila Airport. However, being
overseas Chinese, she was touched by her motherland
culture and language with a spirit of homecoming.

Haipin was excited, yet nervous when she walked through the checkout point. Looking through the waiting line at the arrival gate, she saw a handsome young man anxiously searching for that special someone from the crowd of passengers. As she approached the gate, their eyes met. Then Haipin walked through the gate. They hugged for the first time.

Haipin did not worry about the size of the welcoming party at the airport. It was a weekday and Yan Yun did not want to ask his co-workers at the construction site to lose pay for this occasion. It was summer school also, and his best classmates were in class. Yan Yun, therefore, was the one-man welcoming party there to greet the young lady from the Philippines. Actually, Haipin was more comfortable chatting with her long-time dream guy without the curious stares from his friends.

Haipin's first impression of Yan Yun was good. The young man was slim, with average body build and a tan look. However, he had sort of a weird way of dressing. Instead of western style dress, suitable for formal social activity, Yan Yun wore yellow college student jacket and blue jeans (pants for working people). Haipin thought he was a genius that labeled his status as a college senior, and a temporary summer construction worker wearing informal dress in such a strange way.

Spring Comes to the Alley

Yan Yun and Haipin rode a taxi from the airport to his one room living facility. This was the first time in years that Yan Yun did not ride a bus or his bicycle home. Taxi drivers usually knew how to make more tips by judging the customer and the luggage.

"Sir, is this beautiful woman your wife? Are you just back from overseas? You must have had a lot of fun on your vacation.   Usually we charge the unoccupied back seats, plus fees for the two big luggage pieces.   For expressing my local hospitality to the sweet young lady, I would like to reduce my rate."

The driver looked at Haipin with a smile as he opened the car door and unloaded luggage from the trunk. Haipin thought it might be her luck to pick up a well-mannered driver. In addition to paying regular mileage charges for the taxi, Haipin handed the driver a red envelope as an additional tip. In Chinese tradition, money in a red envelope is a gift, and the value of the gift is usually more than fixed fees.

As the taxicab stopped at the end of the narrow alley, some curious adults and kids next door came to see what happened with the single Yan Yun with a young woman. In history, there were more ambulance and police cars visiting here than that of taxi cabs.

Neighbors wondered how some one here could afford to pay a taxicab.

Haipin did not have a bad impression about the new residence environment here in Taipei. She was born and grew up in similar crowded narrow streets in Manila. The differences might be with the economic background of the alley population. There was no business firm, small or big; there was no family earning average income, that is, simply a low-income working class neighborhood. Haipin, on the contrary, had many business neighbors and her parents ran a profitable shipping agency. She enjoyed a good mid-class family life.

In Haipins's mind she understood that this was Yan Yun's first time since he left the Army to rent a room for daily life. For many years he moved from one place to another, staying at a warehouse space or a friend's living room with a portable bed or on the floor just for a temporary overnight stay. Yan Yun might be very happy to finally live in a private room.

At the same time Yan Yun was concerned whether Haipin could survive this kind of poor accommodations. The room was upstairs, a small room without doors. The windows were always open for lack of air conditioning. Mosquitoes and other bugs were common in most families. There was only one trench toilet shared by several families. If there was anything good, the room had no hallway to access next door residents. There were no windows opening to people around. At least minimum privacy was provided.

Everyday was a working day for Yan Yun, the work-study student and army veteran. He simply did not have much time, money or helping hands to prepare a big welcome party for his fiancée. Haipin understood this. She just liked the quiet setting, a world of just two. Though she had to share doing house chores, such as cooking and laundry, it was kind of a new experience, an independent life without the maids.

Though Yan Yun did not prepare a special party for this occasion, ironically someone did for Haipin, but with bad manners. As Yan Yun and Haipin returned home from grocery shopping, they found the desk drawer in which important documents and currency were stored was not properly closed. Then they found Haipin's jewelry and currency was missing. It was a total saving through years of her hard work. Haipin wished to help financially as much as she could with her fiancée's college education. She also needed money for her search for employment in her new country.

The unexpected loss of her savings, though disappointing to her starting a new life in a new land, Haipin kept her good spirits on the outlook of a happy life in the future. She planned to get married, then the couple would put their best efforts into searching for employment. At that time, Yan Yun was a college senior, a semester away from earning a Bachelor's degree. Haipin held an Associate's degree in elementary education with a teaching certificate. She had confidence that both of them had a good chance in finding jobs. Though it could take time to secure employment, Haipin was optimistic about their future careers. At present she did not feel uncomfortable living at the poor narrow alley, believing that for determined minds, the poor alley was as rich soil for seeding the spring blooming. People would not like to live there forever, of course, but think of a better life elsewhere.

The Lost Blessing

The immediate project, the big one, in Haipin's mind was to prepare a wedding. Yan Yun was even more eager to take the vow. First they considered parental permission; their presence was great for this occasion. Unfortunately however, it was not a reality. The 1949 Chinese Civil War had totally cut off Yan Yun's communication with his parents. Haipin did not expect her mom to change her mind regarding Haipin's choice any time soon.

They could not find helpful assistance from friends. They needed volunteer workers and finance sources as well. In the absence of outside help, the couple decided to make things simple. Haipin would work on most of the preparation. She did not print fancy wedding invitations; sending postcards instead. Yan Yun would invite less than two dozen friends for the wedding. The big help came from the church and generous hearted friends.

A Catholic priest kindly conducted the wedding ceremony and provided church facilities free for this ritual service. Yan Yun was excited on the wedding day, wearing a used dress suit borrowed from a friend. For the bride, Haipin did not have many choices. She must either buy a new bridal gown or get one from a rental store. She chose the rental. Saving money, rather than dress design was in the mind of the once mid-class family's spoiled girl.

Both families of the bride and bridegroom were missing at the ceremony. Yan Yun lost contact with his parents since he joined the government army during the Chinese Communists' 'liberation war'. Haipin did not wish to let her mother know what was about to happen. Therefore two couples from friends were chosen to take the parents' places for the wedding.

The wedding was held on a Sunday morning. They hoped friends could come. About 20 guests greeted the newlyweds. The guests were basically the groom's college classmates, his current co-workers at the construction site, and some former army comrades. But the couple missed most the caring and warm blessings from their beloved parents.

The banquet is an important part at a wedding. For people who could financially afford this it would be as lavish and luxurious as possible. The young couple was in a bad financial situation. They did not have any bank savings. Banks would not make loans to people who did not have a permanent employment income. Haipin and Yan Yun finally decided to provide an economical lunch at a restaurant, opposed to the traditional 10-course formal banquet menu. They worried about the number of unexpected guests that would add more tables and make their budget out of control. Yan Yun never forgot his friend, S. S. Bao, who brought with him a $1,000 NT as reserve fund in case additional tables were needed. The reserve fund was never used because the number of guests for the banquet was smaller than originally planned.

The wedding day was just another day in the groom's busy life. Yan Yun, after the wedding, wearing work clothing with heavy boots and metal bonnet started the next day at the construction site. While Haipin, not thinking about the honeymoon, but worked hard in the search for a job. With school teaching experience and valid government teaching certificate, she targeted a career in elementary education. Since Yan Yun would earn his college degree next semester, the newlywed couple gave up the expenses of a honeymoon, pursuing instead a productive and money saving career of job hunting and career planning.

Behind the Smile

Though Haipin was born and grew up in the Philippines, the Chinese ethnicity of her parents and her own college education in a Chinese language school in Manila had made her confident of having a good career on the Chinese soil. She was optimistic about finding a good job without a big problem.

This optimistic outlook began to turn sour as she sent job applications and walked in personnel offices. Government bureaucratic red tape was the obstacle of getting anything to progress smoothly. Another common problem in most underdeveloped counties at that time was personal influence over legal interpretation. Rules and regulations could be applied in favor of personal view of the bureaucrat. The best way to get results in favor of the one seeking help was by bribe. Haipin did not have money or human resources to do this. She tried to believe that not all bureaucrats were bad.

Assuming that the Overseas Chinese Affairs, a government agency responsible for providing assistance to Chinese from foreign countries would be a good place to go for help, Haipin one day walked into the office building. She had a good conversation with an employment counselor expressing her interest in looking for an elementary school teaching position. The official seemed very nice, smiling all the time.

"Certainly your application will be placed on the priority list. We do offer overseas Chinese special placement service. At the same time, you should pursue other sources, such as private schools, or positions in business. Remember we are required to place our school teaching program graduates first."

Again, the counselor assured Haipin that his office would do the best to place her in a city school. She would be notified by mail in case an opening that would best fit her qualifications became available.

The warm acceptance from the counselor made Haipin believe she had a good chance to secure city school employment ahead. She waited for the good news from the Overseas Affairs Office. Meanwhile she tried to learn some school activities such as instruction, textbooks, and extra curricula in local schools. She sometimes stopped kids on their way home from school asking what they were doing today. Occasionally she invited neighbor school children to her apartment talking about the fun of going to school. Apparently this was Haipin's early preparation for assuming her teaching job.

For several weeks Hapin had not heard anything from the placement service of the Overseas Chinese Affairs since her contact with the counselor. The new school year would start in less than two months. She worried about her chance to get a job before classes began. Haipin then visited the placement office in person. She was disappointed to find out that all teaching positions in the city schools were filled. A few vacancies still open were small schools in remote mountain villages. The disadvantages of teaching in small rural schools were transportation and living accommodations.

The placement office did not promise that Haipin could fill any of the remaining vacancies. She remembered how nice the counselor was and his promise to her at her initial contact with the agency. She did not understand things behind the official's smile. However she was devastated in not being able to find a job. Haipin reluctantly asked for help from her former college teachers in Taipei who were visiting guest professors at the Chinese College in Manila. Haipin earned her teaching degree at that college.

A couple of weeks prior to classes beginning for the new school year, Haipin received a teaching contract issued by the Education Office of Taipei County. She was appointed to fill a position in a small rural school in the mountain region where most of the residents worked at the coal mining company.

The Snoring Hogs

It was apparently human relations that helped make this appointment possible. The professor who made recommendation to the placement counselor for Haipin's appointment was an influential person in the academic society. Haipin did not wish to wait any longer in order to find a city school position. She accepted the appointment.

The small mining village, Yu Fon, had a population of about 2000. The majority worked for the local Coal Company. Others were farmers. The community was very proud of their school. The relationship between teacher and parents was extremely good. The student body was less than 100, composed of six grades, from first through sixth.

The transportation was a big problem for Haipin's commute to work from her residence in Taipei, to the rural small village. It would take two hours to get there. She did not have any other choice but to find a room or a space there.

Unfortunately the school did not provide apartments for its staff. Some teachers lived in homes of friends and relatives. Others rented rooms in nearby villages. Haipin's situation was unique; she was the only female teacher who had to travel two hours one way by railroad, bus, and walk. The community was willing to offer helping hands welcoming the young woman. It was no doubt that Hapin got special attention. She was an overseas Chinese, born and raised in Manila, thus the community treated her very well. Furthermore teachers held a respectable status of all professionals in long Chinese history.

Haipin was one of the six professionals on the teaching staff, and she needed help the most. Households really did not have available spare space for renting. However residents would like to support their local school and school teachers, especially the one teacher from the Philippines. Finally one of the families offered a space for Haipin. The parents who made living space available to her felt a sense of pride.

Since raising hogs could make additional income for the mining or farming family, almost every household raised hogs. Some families could afford to build outdoor pens for the pigs, others simply raised pigs in the kitchen, or bedroom. Pigs were confined in a bamboo pen next to the kitchen table all day. It was the first time for Haipin, once a successful businessman's spoiled daughter, to live in such an unsanitary environment. Besides the bad smell, Haipin was not comfortable with the noise of pigs snoring. During the first couple of months, Haipin did not have a single night of good sleep. The pig's snoring at midnight frequently woke her up. She was alone. She wished to share her feelings with Yan Yun. She decided not to do so because he was a poor student and there was no way he could change the situation. She wished to call her mother, but she would say, 'it was your choice.' She could not quit the respectable teaching position to become a jobless public welfare recipient. At this point her only expectation was to sacrifice now and enjoy life in the near future. Since all residents in this community could live happily, why did she have to be excluded.

Walking Barefoot

Besides the lack of modern utilities, such as running water, electricity, natural gas in households and schools, Haipin was surprised to see people walking barefoot. She could not find many of her third grade class pupils wearing shoes. The warm weather might not bother these kids walking without shoes, but the mountain trails that they traveled to school were gravel, muddy, and had a lot of plant pricks. Since there was no school bus available, students walked back and forth to school on foot; the long walking distance might be five miles or so.

As for her teaching environment, Haipin had no complaints under such a rural setting. Being a devoted early child teacher, she enjoyed working with these less material minded, but obedient kids. They respected the teacher. Following the model set by their parents who worked hard in the coal mine or the rice paddy, kids in Haipin's class worked diligently on class assignments without a thought of cheating. Sometimes her students would bring homemade food to the beloved teacher. Parents occasionally would invite Haipin as their guest for dinner. The parents wanted to know how their kid's learning performance was in the class. They also liked very much to hear Haipin's stories about her family and life in the Philippines.

Teachers were required to have a kid's learning performance conference with parents by visiting the student's home at least once a semester. In some cases, if the student had a learning or behavior problem, more family visits were scheduled. Some students lived in small villages in the hills or mountain passes which made passage difficult. As Haipin traveled on foot to meet the parents, she realized how uncomfortable for the farmers, and especially the kids, to walk barefoot from one place to another. She did not think families had first aid medicine for treating injuries. Haipin also realized there was no ambulance vehicle that could reach these areas.

Haipin, once a metropolitan girl, was curious as to how kids with bare feet behaved in sports and other activities on the playground. She noticed that all kids in her class, with shoes on or not, showed very little difference as far as comfort in physical activity, such as running. This must be the nature that gives our human bodies the ability to survive. Haipin also noticed parents' wishes for their kids was not much different than other classmates wearing shoes. Some kids brought shoes to school and put them on while on campus, but took them off on the way home.

Though the majority of the population in local communities still spoke their dialect, all instructions conducted in school required that it be in the nation's official language, Chinese Mandarin. Some naughty pupils using local dialect would make jokes about Haipin's teaching style, or what she was wearing. They assumed that their foreign born teacher would not understand what they said.

The kids were stunned when Haipin would smile at their jokes. However they still doubted her ability to understand local dialect. Once Haipin stopped their bad language usage in school by using local dialect; then all students worked hard to avoid using language other than standard Chinese Mandarin.

Tasting Better, Feeling Better

The fall semester was over. Haipin wished to have a chance to move out from the rural mining village, so she could participate in cultural activities in the city and see her husband more often. However, she realized the possibility was very slim. In general, most openings are available in the fall semester which begins a new school year. She, like other staff, had signed an annual teaching contract with the county government for her current job location.

It was hard to believe that Haipin was informed of a new position which opened at a small school, Wan Li Elementary, under the same Taipei County jurisdiction. Even though the school is surrounded by hills in three directions, it is located near a water resort area, Kingsan Beach Creation Center. The busy highway leads to the beach facility right in front of the Wan Li Elementary School. For teachers in the mountain region rural schools, Wan Li School is one of the most preferred choices among teachers. Haipin was asked by the Taipei County Education Office if she would consider a transfer. She thought if this was not a miracle, then what was it? The highway would give easier access to Taipei, the capital where her husband still worked and attended college. This was the first improvement in her career and life after marriage.

When Haipin began spring semester on her new job at Wan Li Elementary School, Yan Yun was closer to earning his Bachelor of Arts degree in May. He had reason to look ahead to a better life, instead of a student who never made enough for the family, and who most of the time stayed home alone. He went from on the move hustle and bustle to a daily routine and a newly wed warm family. A college degree could provide prosperity and better living accommodations.

The commencement ceremony was not only Yan Yun's big day, but after four years of studying hard, he finally would receive a college degree; it was also a big day for Haipin, the student wife. Unfortunately for some reason, parents of Yan Yun and Haipin were absent. Yan Yun did not expect that his friends would visit the campus from quite a long distance. Thus, at this celebration, Haipin played multiple roles; as a graduate's spouse, substitute parents of both families, and friends as well.

With a college degree in hand, Yan Yun began to search for employment immediately after leaving the campus. It was summer, 1965, the new school year was just about to begin. Many personnel changes would be done before classes started. It was really the best time for the new college graduate to look for a position on campuses. Yan Yun worked as hard as he could to search for a teaching job. He mailed many applications to schools located in cities and rural communities as well. He began to doubt his chances in finding school employment as time approached the end of August. He then used more aggressive ways to do the search. Yan Yun visited with the personnel offices in targeted schools. This tactic did not work either. He was tired of hearing the personal director's kind rejection words, 'we will inform you if a vacancy becomes available for you.'

Yan Yun's hopes for a new job seemed doomed. Meanwhile, Haipin did all she could to help the frustrated husband. Learning from her previous job searching experience in Taipei, Haipin tried the human resource approach again. She asked her former college teacher, then a university professor at the Taiwan Teachers' University for help. A week before classes began, Yan Yun got a call from the Principal of Keelung City 5th Junior High regarding a full time position as a 7th grade English and homeroom teacher. Apparently it was the professor's recommendation to the junior high that made Yan Yun's appointment possible.

The security of a new job for Yan Yun gave Haipin much needed release of her financial burden as well as her feeling of loneliness at home. They rented a tiny room in the City of Keelung where Yan Yun's new employer was located. The city, in northern Taiwan, was a seaport without modern utilities at that time. One could hardly find paved streets. Air and water pollution gave the city a bad name, 'dark seaport.' A large portion of the population was fisherman. Another large group of residents was shipyard labor workers.

Haipin rode a commute bus line to and from work, about two hours round trip, while Yan Yun had to climb on foot half an hour one way to reach his teaching facility located on a hill. Like the majority of the population, the couple owned a bicycle for short distance transportation.

For Haipin this was a new change, a feeling of stability and a kind of settling down. Though the one room living space was too small to be comfortable, they could not think of anything better under such tight budget circumstances. They shared a kitchen, bath space, and toilet with the landlord. Believe it or not, the landlord's family always had priority to use the facilities at any anytime. Haipin's worst experience with the property owner was the less than friendly conduct shown by their family members, the teenage kids. Teachers hold a respectable position in Chinese history. However, there was no guarantee that the low paid teacher would enjoy such social honor in Haipin's current conditions.

The two-paycheck family did not make the couple's life better than average. The schoolteacher was a low paying profession in the heavily military spending, but low growth wartime economy in Taiwan in the early 1960s. Haipin and Yan Yun were happy to live a peaceful life while starting their careers in this seaport city. They also had a financial plan for the future in mind. Regardless of how difficult it would be to save money, they would avoid temptation when buying food and clothing. The motivation for saving was to have a bank account that could be used in an emergency. Things on their mind were to have kids and to support career change.

The food budget was hard to control in an average family. People consider good food as part of a good life. Since Keelung was a fishing port, seafood dominated the food market. Fish was cheaper and became a household plate on the dining table; while beef, pork, and poultry would be an addition to the dinner table for families earning above average income. Chicken was the most expensive at that time.

Having above average income, Haipin enjoyed a happy family life with her husband. The couple still considered chicken as a very expensive menu item. Their savings in the bank would be zero balances should chicken become the food menu on the table every day. After serious consideration, they made an alternative choice; that was, to buy not the whole chicken, but a part of it once a week. When Haipin got to the chicken cutting board counter in the nearby farmer's market, the butcher handed her the chicken and smiled,

'Teacher, here is yours, **a quarter of it!**'

It became a routine purchase pattern, Haipin always asking the butcher for this quantity.

After years of uncertainty of her future; marriage, employment and moving around, Haipin was beginning to feel secure. She was no longer a student's wife, but an equal part of a loving family. Life was wonderful and the taste of chicken was really great.

THREE

On the Way to America

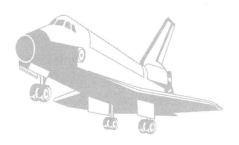

Chapter Three

The F-2 Hassle

Since Hapin settled down in the harbor city of Keelung and said 'bye-bye' to the status of a student wife, she enjoyed very much the peaceful life with abundance. A good job, a sweet husband in the same profession, plenty of seafood, and an occasional taste of pork or chicken. On Sunday, a holiday, or semester break, she would ride the family bicycle and go sightseeing at the seashore, watching fishing boats and cargo ships go in and out of the harbor.

A bicycle became a personal transportation necessity at that time. It made it easier for a person who might not like walking on foot for some distance. Haipin seemed to have confidence in her husband's skills in operating the bike. Instead of grasping Yan Yun from his back for safety, she always sat on the back seat of the bike, reading a book. One unexpected fall from the bike changed her family plan. This accident ended the couple's plan to have a child. Haipin had a miscarriage with her three-month pregnancy.

To take advantage of easing the temporary urgent needs of finance and time for nursing a baby, Yan Yun decided to advance his education to another level. He would like to pursue a graduate program with a Master's degree in mind. This time he targeted a graduate school, not in local Taiwan, but in the United States. Thus Haipin would have no choice but to become a student wife again.

Her husband's academic goal in earning degrees in the United States was far more expensive than planning to have a child in Taiwan. There were two big problems facing the young couple. One was funding for graduate education; the other was to get a passport from the government and a visa from the U.S. embassy in Taipei as well.

Yan Yun worked hard quietly for a while on getting admission from a university in the United States and his government's permit to study overseas. The result was quite optimistic. Southeast Missouri State College in Cape Girardeau had admitted him to a Master's degree program, starting with the fall 1967 academic year. Together with the admission paper, he also found the Immigration and Naturalization Service form I-20, an official document for a foreign student to get a U.S. visa. On the finance requirement, the college asked for $1,500 as the first year expenses. A student must show a bank check of this amount at the U. S. Custom Office when entering the U.S.

Besides U.S. university admissions paper, the government in Taipei (Republic of China) would issue a permit to a qualified student for an overseas education program. One of the tough requirements to obtain this permit was to pass an overseas education examination.

Yan Yun was very lucky because he successfully passed the test on his first try.

Being a spouse, Haipin, though having reluctance in leaving her teaching job and facing possible hardship in America, had no intention of disappointing her husband's ambitions for a better future by the attainment of an advanced college education. She thus committed herself to support Yan Yun by any means possible in contributing to his big education endeavor adventure.

Haipin never believed that she could raise any significant amount for her husband's education. She however wished to do her best by exhausting resources that could turn positive. She sold her jewelry, which was left after the burglary. Again she asked her former college professor, then Dean of Instruction at the National Taiwan Teachers University in Taipei for a loan. The respectable and caring professor did generously make an endowment and loan for Yan Yun's education fund, totaling $500. The three sources (jewelry, donation, and loan) made up two thirds of the $1,500 required by Southeast Missouri State College. Haipin was glad that Yan Yun secured an $800 loan from his former military friend, and $200 gifts from public school colleagues. Thus the finance requirement was met.

The next big task facing Haipin had nothing to do with money, but it was an equally important part of going to the United States, and that was to get a student's spouse visa, F2. To further education studies in the United States was students' top choice in Taiwan in the 50's and 60s. To get an F1 visa was a popular chatting topic among college seniors. The United States granted F visa for foreign students. F1 was for an individual student. The spouse of the student if approved would get an F2 visa. Although the United States did not set many restrictions for applying for an F2 visa, a student spouse from Taiwan could still face tough inquiry. Many students from Taiwan, while living with a spouse, would stay in the United States after leaving school. The United States wanted students to return to their homeland after graduation.

The Taiwan government (Republic of China) had tough eligibility requirements for the issuing of a passport to the spouse of a student. One of the provisions was time requirement. The student must live in the United States at least two years with proof of employment or a bank account that could support a year's expense living in the United States.

Being a work-study student with full-time employment Yan Yun was lonesome. He did not have a social life. He needed his wife sharing love and care with him. After the end of his first semester in graduate school, he asked Haipin to quit her teaching job and come to the United States.

Under one of the current government regulations for applying for a married student passport, Haipin must delay making application until her husband's two-year eligibility requirement was met.

The pressure on Haipin to quit her job and to fight to get a passport was somewhat high. She too, eagerly wished to enjoy family life with her husband. Thus, she made up her mind and quit her current teaching job, even at the risk of the uncertainty of getting employment soon. It was a shock to her colleagues to know that Haipin would leave teaching halfway through the school year. However, they congratulated her for her prosperous life in the United States.

For traveling overseas Haipin needed to get a passport from the government of the Republic of China (Taiwan) and F2 Visa from the U.S. embassy in Taipei. She quietly contacted friends who knew about government bureaucracy on the issuing of a passport. Unfortunately, the government would not allow the spouse of a student to reunite with a husband or wife under the current regulations, unless the two-year time requirement was met. Haipin got her first setback.

She then contacted the American Embassy in Taipei for a visa. One of the embassy employees kindly advised her not to file an application unless she had a valid passport. Should Haipin have a rejection on file as the employee indicated, she could have more difficulty applying for a visa later.

The setback did not keep Haipin from giving up her hard work toward success. This time she took advantage of the government's special assistance programs on overseas Chinese living in Taiwan. Through her friends who had connection with the Overseas Affairs Agency, she learned that the assistance program would not work on her case. The government was concerned with the well being of students living in foreign countries. A two-year time requirement was a kind of assurance that students would secure employment and build bank accounts.

Haipin seemed to be losing direction as how to obtain a U.S. visa. So far she had exhausted all sources available to help her. She was depressed because of unemployment too. Haipin regretted her stupid decision to file for resignation early. The delay of getting a visa had tremendous pressure on the couple's daily life.

The Smiling Mom

The seemingly helpless Haipin was deeply frustrated. Considering it might take months to get a U.S. visa, she decided to visit her mother in Manila. It might be a proper time to mend the relationship with her mother after her marriage to Yan Yun a couple of years ago.

Mother gave Haipin a warm welcome. Mom's first smile warmed Haipin's heart and released her feeling of guilt. Mother was to no longer make negative comments about Yan Yun, but, instead talk about living in the United States. Haipin could sense her mother's pride while chatting about the young couple's future in

America. Deep in her heart, mother seemed to have high expectations for her daughter and son-in-law.

In Manila, Haipin's neighborhood where she spent her childhood had a social world that was greater than what she had in Taiepi. Through her parents' business associates, Haipin could get assistance from many human resources. For example, several known travel agencies in Manila in general, and her neighboring residence area in particular, always advised her family how to contact the government. Any petitions that went through the inner circle of the government bureaucracy would get better results. Haipin wished to find new channels to get a U.S. visa. Apparently the new prosperity never had been better here.

The financial support from Haipin's friends and her mom's business associates boosted the frustrated young woman into having an optimistic outlook for getting a U.S. visa. One travel agency, after being rewarded a better commission fee, offered Haipin a guarantee to get a U.S. visa. The agency considered this case as a good case for winning. The big advantage was Haipin's passport. She did not need to apply for a new passport from the Philippine government. She held a valid passport issued by the Chinese government (Taiwan) for an overseas Chinese citizen. The travel agency simply sent her Chinese passport to the American embassy in Manila for a tourist visa.

It took quite some time to get a response from the travel agency. The American Consulate in Manila was reviewing Haipin's application. Since Yan Yun came to the United States holding a student visa issued by the American Embassy in Taipei, the consulate office wished to know why Haipin, living in Taipei, did not get a visa from a U. S. Consulate in the same country.

After a month long investigation, the Taipei office cleared Haipin's application file. The American Embassy in Manila was notified that Haipin did not file application for a visa in any American consulate office in Taiwan. There was no record of rejection. It meant that Haipin's application was being processed for approval.

Haipin was excited over such good news. She expressed her appreciation for the hard work that the travel agency did on her behalf. As the official document (U.S. visa endorsement) reached her, it was unthinkable that the good news turned out not to be that good. It was a tourist visa. Haipin could only stay in the United States for six months with the possibility of a one-year extension. She wished she could stay in America as long as her husband did.

It was actually some of her friends who were knowledgeable on visa application and did not want her to hold a tourist visa. They convinced Haipin that she should be qualified to apply for a student spouse endorsement credential, that was, an F2 visa. For an F2 visa bearer, Haipin's eligibility for continuous extension after the expiration day, meant she could stay in the United States with Yan Yun as long as he maintained student status.

Is Money Everything?

It was another setback, another frustration, and another time consuming effort for the young woman. Haipin now was fighting to get an F2 visa. Could the tourist endorsement help her get a student spouse visa?

Not really sure, Haipin then launched another big attempt on the visa matter. Her goal was to make a change from tourist endorsement to a student visa. She initiated a campaign to motivate friends in supporting her efforts. The campaign did result in getting a clue on how to contact influential individuals who had employee friends working at the visa section of the Consulate. Several weeks passed without success.

One year was long enough for Yan Yun to live alone in a foreign land supporting himself by working for minimum wage, doing cooking and laundry at home, and doing studies and research at the college. Haipin could not wait any longer. She planned to unite with her husband in the United States prior to a new academic year beginning at the end of August. She then went back to the travel agency for help.

The travel agency, being in business for decades, had a reputation for successfully getting travel documents on difficult situations. They did have a lot of experience in handling special cases on applying for passports, visa and health certificates. However the travel agency would not guarantee the success, even though a high commission fee could be charged.

Though the travel agency did not guarantee success, Haipin decided to take a chance. Her decision was not easy to make. She heard rumors that her previous approved visa could be cancelled if evidence to support changing status was invalid. That means she could lose the tourist endorsement without replacing it with another visa. Worst of all was that a rejection in a local U.S. Consulate could make her application be denied by American visa issuing offices around the world.

Before giving up applying for an F2 visa, Haipin made the last effort by consulting the travel agency again, preparing to pay the highest cost within her ability if the agency could find alternative ways to a success trial.

Finally, on behalf of her request, the travel agency agreed to work on the visa class change again. Haipin handed her visa to the agency and made an additional deposit for this project. The agency immediately softened their stand by saying that the petition had a good chance of getting approved. Haipin was convinced by their strong focus on her case. Several very experienced old hands were assigned on this mission. In her mind she believed for a fact, that just like a powerful lawyer, he cannot change the law, but he could best interpret the law and win the case.

Haipin got a telephone call from the agency about 10 days after turning in her documents. She could not believe her ears, but the voice was clear:

' Haipin, congratulations! Come and pick up
your visa with the new endorsement, F2.'

The once depressed young woman turned frustration into optimism as she hung up the telephone. She was overjoyed on the reality that her dream to unite with her husband would become true: not a year, not a month, but within a couple of weeks. She hugged everyone at home that moment. It was really a great moment. Haipin was moved by her mother's smile. Mom seldom expressed a good mood toward her since her marriage to Yan Yun.

The Cheering Crowd

Haipin never thought she could have a chance to go to America. With the success in getting a U.S. visa, the journey to a great country, the land of opportunity was just about to begin. She felt so lucky that she was married to a wonderful guy. Despite his busy work-study schedule in the foreign land, Yan Yun still kept sending her airmail regularly.

The unbelievable caring effort that her husband had made to Haipin could be found by his hard work in saving money. Besides classes at Southeast Missouri State College, Yan Yun worked full time off campus at below minimum wage from $.70 to $2.00 per hour (in

71

1968). Within a short time (less than a year), he could send $600 to Haipin for her travel expenses on the road to St. Louis, Missouri.

As Haipin's departure to the United States drew closer, her best friends planned a farewell party, wishing her a safe trip and celebrating her new life in America. According to the plan, a lunch would be served at a Chinese restaurant on the departure day. All partygoers were welcomed to go the airport shaking hands with Haipin at the terminal.

Finally the day came. Haipin would fly the Philippine Airline from Manila to St. Louis, Missouri on the 30th of May, 1968. All members of the farewell lunch party gathered at the restaurant. People who did not plan to come surprised Haipin. Sister Maria arrived at the airport form Davao City, just three hours before the flight departure. A college classmate went to the airport on her lunch hour. However, Haipin could not believe that only Louis, her elder brother from home came to the party. Mother, being a manager of the family shipping business, seldom left her duty for social activity. She did hug her daughter when Haipin said goodbye and left home.

Besides friends and family members at the luncheon party at the airport, Haipin also met some of her school colleagues who took time off from teaching. As she walked through the boarding gate, people in the crowd waved hands with a smile. This cheering spirit was quite contrary to the low profile she flew to Taipei with a couple of years ago.

Haipin began a new journey on the way to America on a mission as a student wife, just as she did in Taipei.

FOUR

Wow! The Immense, Beautiful Lands

CHAPTER FOUR

The Feeling of Being Welcomed

It was Haipin's first long flight across the Pacific Ocean; she was excited and curious. Early in her childhood, she knew a little about the United States as a wonderland. In the wonderland, kids enjoyed visiting the big zoo, going to the park and playing with new toys; some she never imagined, and seeing mile long railroad trains whistling across the open field. Now, as an adult and student wife she would live with her husband in this wonderland, enjoying a happy family life.

During the flight on board the airplane, Haipin remembered the warmth of friendship given her by the friendly smiling faces at the airport. She was looking forward to seeing her husband; she could not wait for the first hug, after missing him for almost a year.

Haipin was so excited; she could hardly believe she had the chance to fulfill her childhood dream to see the United States. If it was not a miracle, then, it must be her luck: the luck of marrying a hard working young man, and the luck of having an opportunity to come to the United States.

In the 1960s, the government (the Republic of China in Taiwan) allowed students to study abroad for advanced college degrees. Most students favored graduate schools in the United States. However, only a small portion of them had made it. A successful student must get admission from an American college, must pass a government Study Abroad Examination, and must meet financial requirements. Based on Yan Yun's financial hardship, no one could believe he had a chance to study abroad. Haipin was proud of her husband's determination and continued struggle in getting her to the United States.

As the captain announced to the passengers to prepare for landing in Hawaii, Haipin, through the aircraft window, saw a group of islands. It was not strange for a person from island countries like the Philippines and Taiwan to see familiar scenes of islands and ocean. Haipin, however, had a special feeling this time. This is Hawaii, a gateway to the mainland United States.

As Haipin got out of the airplane and stepped on the American soil, she was excited over this familiar scene, but in a new place. The weather in Hawaii in May was just as warm as that of Manila, and the colorful tropical botanic gardens were also familiar. Walking in the port entry, the U.S. Customs Service, she was surprised by the multi-language 'welcome' signs in English, Chinese, and Japanese. The Customs staff was also multi-cultural. Caucasian faces, mixed with Asian employees could be seen in the big hall. Since the majority of travelers were from Asian countries, faces of Orientals were everywhere in the airport. At this point, Haipin did not have the feeling of a foreigner. Although she did not have friends or relatives to welcome her at the airport, she was not alone. Neither did many of the travelers have friends in Hawaii. The smiling faces of the Customs employees, and the welcome signs made her feel welcome. It was the east meeting the west.

Haipin's luggage passed the check-in station easily. None of the luggage and handbags had been opened for inspection. Probably people holding an F2 visa were less suspicious by the customs officials for sneaking commercial and illegal articles into the United States. For this consideration she was glad, as a student's wife.

A couple of hours after landing in Los Angeles International Airport, Haipin flew United Airlines for a domestic flight to the heartland of America - Saint Louis, Missouri. Here was another landscape of the United States. During the almost three hour flight she kept looking out the window, viewing the horizon where the sky meets the earth. Instead of Haipin's familiar scene of islands, big and small, surrounded by an ocean, as she used to see in the Philippines and Taiwan, now she had a new picture of inland America: mountains, hills, rivers, lakes, highways, and vast open fields. The huge land of America impressed her, and she said, *'Wow, the immense beautiful lands*!

The Blooming Roses

Haipin did not think anything could ruin her good spirits while thinking of the welcome party at the Saint Louis Airport terminal. Her husband's transportation relied on bus travel or a friend's vehicle for the 120 mile, one way trip from Cape Girardeau. There might be out of control things, such as a vehicle problem or change in the bus schedule. Haipin would feel helpless and alone at the airport in a strange city. She prayed that things would turn out for the best.

Her worry faded away immediately while walking from the boarding gate. Among the waiting crowd, she noticed her husband's smiling face and waving hands. Along, side by side with Yan Yun, was another young gentleman smiling at her. It was a sign of a very warm welcome. She immediately had a sense of confidence, safety and security.

Tom introduced himself to Haipin.

"Welcome, Haipin, I am Tom. Yan Yun is my classmate. He works hard in class and outside campus employment as well. You are a lovely young lady."

Then, Yan Yun and Haipin got to Tom's car and headed south to Cape Girardeau. It was a 250-mile round trip between Saint Louis and the college campus. Haipin thanked Tom for his help. Tom took a day off from his part-time job especially for this trip. He paid for the gasoline too.

Tom was a Caucasian in Yan Yun's history class. They had seats side by side in the classroom. It was Yan Yun's first semester in an American college. He got some needed help from Tom in taking notes from the professor's lectures.

Though Haipin was tired after long hours of international and domestic flights, plus another three hours sitting in the back seat of a car, she still maintained a good mood. Being a native of Missouri, Tom told interesting stories about the cities and towns alongside the highway. He acted as a tour guide for the young lady from a foreign country. Meanwhile, Haipin noticed that American people are very proud of their cities. They advertise their communities' history, sports achievements, heroes of local personalities, or special features on the bulletin board at the city limit. Travelers would have some idea about the city when entering the community. Male travelers might smile at 'City of Beautiful Women' signs. Here comes a city honored with a given flower. As the party approached its destination, Cape Girardeau, the sign ' City of Roses' seemed to welcome the guests. Haipin immediately sensed it was going to be roses everywhere. She would live in a community as beautiful as a rose garden.

Haipin walked into the two-room apartment that Yan Yun had lived in for almost a year. The first impression was the roses in full bloom at the fence. Then it was the beautiful green lawn around house. Yan Yun shared bath, toilet, and living room with the owner, who was a retired lady from Germany. Instantly Haipin liked the small house. It was located at 402 Frederic St. on a hill with dense shaded trees, and of course, colorful roses. Compared to apartments and farmers' houses where she resided in Taiwan, this residence, furnished with mattress beds, gas oven, air-conditioning and heating, electricity, and running water, was sort of a luxury living quarter she enjoyed for the first time. Yes, for the first time she had a private family telephone. Another convenience for this location was the short walking distance to the college campus, a post office across the street, a grocery story two blocks away, a shoe factory (Yan Yun's off-campus employer), and the large city rose garden was several miles away.

Haipin's first week as a student wife in the United States was to try to become familiar with her new environment as soon as possible. The first thing on her mind was the transportation. Though it was of medium size, Cape Girardeau at that time, had no public transportation. Prior to her coming to this country, she learned, that in the United States, driving a car was not something of a luxury, but a necessity. She and Yan Yun began to work hard, saving to buy a car. Before they could secure an auto loan from a local bank, they went everywhere on foot.

The young foreign student couple was warmly welcomed in this college town. Because the student population from foreign countries on the college campus was relatively small, as compared to large metropolitan universities, some local residents were curious about other cultures. Very often a passing car would stop and the driver would ask a foreign student, who was on foot walking to the college campus, or to and from the grocery store if they would like a ride. Haipin appreciated this kind, caring 'southern hospitality'.

Yan Yun left home for America a couple of months prior to his third anniversary with Haipin. Now it was early May. They were reunited again. Their fourth anniversary fell on October 25th. The young couple considered celebrating their fourth anniversary early this year by taking advantage of Yan Yun's several week semester break. Haipin could use these job searching days as a pre-employment vacation.

The Love/ Hate of Owning a Car

On top of their list of urgent things requiring adjustment to life in the United States, was to own a car. Since driving a car is part of American life, Yan Yun and Haipin eagerly wanted to own their personal transportation soon. Without a car there could be no vacation, and the spirits of their anniversary might be ruined. They also needed a car to find employment. Though Haipin did not learn to operate a bicycle in Taiwan, she hoped she could be a good driver in the United States.

What was also worrisome was the bank loan. Haipin did not have a job yet, while her husband's part-time employment income was too small to leave anything for a savings account in the bank. They did not want to wait any longer for savings that could cover the purchase.

The excitement of buying a car pushed the couple hard to find a solution. One day they walked several blocks from their apartment to go window shopping at a used car dealer. Both Yan Yun and Haipin knew nothing about a car. Before going to shop, friends had briefed Yan Yun on things to know about cars, but it was too complicated for the couple to understand; knowing a good car from a bad one. They could not tell the special features of a product made by a given carmaker. What was important was the physical appearance of the car; then came the color and the size.

Every time they walked in the used car dealership lot, the salesman would welcome them with less than a business smile on choosing a car, but more of a curiosity about where the young couple came from and what academic program they were working on at the college. They probably believed that most foreign students could not afford to buy a car. The salesman did not want to waste his time on window shopping customers. For example, one salesman imitated the accent of Yan Yun's conversation in English. Haipin did not believe it was a good practice to use someone's accent as jokes for selling merchandise.

There were too many cars to choose from. If Haipin trusted the sales person, every car was good. They would only compare the quality of a car by the price. Since finance played a big role in buying a car, Haipin and Yan Yun did not see much hope in owning a car soon.

The dilemma went on for a week. They needed a car, but they did not have savings. Yan Yun's part -time income was too small to put aside any amount for a monthly payment, and Haipin didn't have a job yet. Then, the young couple decided to set a goal of how much they would be able to spend on a car without substantially cutting the food bill, assuming Haipin would find full time employment.

It was their first experience in taking a bold step to try to get something for nothing. They wished to get a bank auto loan without employment or property as security.

One day they walked into a local bank with little expectation, but wishful excitement for a miracle. Since Cape Girardeau is a college town, businesses and residents were accustomed to seeing new student faces from out of town and from foreign countries as well. Surprisingly, Haipin and Yan Yun were getting a warm welcome by a bank employee.

After knowing that the young couple needed a loan to finance the purchase of a used car, the bank did not immediately deny their request, due to their student status. Instead, they dealt with true information. The bank would take under consideration Yan Yun's part-time job income, and the minimum wage Haipin might earn while employed. However, the bank would not determine the value of the loan unless Haipin had detailed information about the car for the loan. She never believed that the bank would consider her future earnings as a base for the loan. Thus, Haipin began to understand what the 'land of opportunity' meant. Instead of rejecting the loan, the bank would take the risk in order to win a potential customer. It makes sense for the business to invest for their future, because Yan Yun was a graduate student with potential to make a good salary after college.

The first part of owning a car seemed in good progress. The bank would consider making a loan available for this purpose. Now they must choose a car; a used car that worked well, but at a low price. It was something that Haipin never thought would be such a time consuming purchase. The young couple did not have much knowledge about the car. However, they were aware that a used car, after years of operation might have defects, such as worn parts. With common sense, they worried that the lower the price of the car the higher the repair cost could be. They needed help from a knowledgeable used car person, but no one was available.

From one used car dealer to another, Haipin and Yan Yun got a lot of 'quality at low price' persuasive statements from salesmen. Though they gained a little knowledge about cars from salesmen, the more confused they became. The more cars they had a chance to see, the more difficulty they had in making a choice. The dilemma went on for several days.

Finally the young couple reached a decision. The blue 1962 Chevrolet, two-door, sedan, a 6 year used car, was their choice. Though the odometer had a number of over 70,000, they did not pay too much attention to the mileage. They believed that the pre-owner might have taken good care of the car. The vehicle seemed in good condition. No peeling paint or damage on the body had been found. The salesman first offered a price of $300. Yan Yun indicated less interest in paying the amount since it was beyond his financial ability. Then, the salesman offered another discount at a total price of $250. Then, the dealership made an additional offer, a free repair within 90 days after sale.

The excitement over owning a car for the first time in their life made the young couple waste no time in putting their signatures on a sales contract. They learned that the car dealership would file the loan papers with the bank on behalf of the borrower. The couple did not even go to the bank. They could choose the monthly payment and the length of the loan. They agreed for a 12-month term, bearing interest of nine percent annually. The car dealer completed the auto registration and tax form with the local and state governments. All the customer had to do was to sign the forms. The couple did not pay a penny to the dealer, but was treated with free coffee, tea, and other refreshments. Haipin did not realize how easy it was to get things done, such as buying a car, in the United States.

Though the owner of the car had changed hands from the car dealer to the young couple, operating the vehicle was not that easy. Before moving the car out of the dealer's lot, a driver's license and auto liability insurance must be in effect. None of the legal documents were available from either Yan Yun or Haipin at that moment. Fortunately, the dealership was willing to deliver the car to Haipin's apartment.

The delivery employee parked the car right in front of the couple's apartment. Since the owners did not know how to operate the vehicle, instead of driving it, they wiped the car frequently with a sense of pride in owning a piece of valuable property. Haipin worried about the security of the car. An unattended vehicle she thought might easily become a target for stealing or vandalism. It was hard to believe that the couple had to walk to buy groceries with a car right in front of the doorstep.

Before they could legally operate the car, either Yan Yun or Haipin must hold a valid driver's license. The auto insurance was another 'must'. Haipin never believed that to buy an insurance policy was not simply paying the premium. The insurance company delayed issuing an insurance card until the primary driver of the car got a valid operator's license. Despite the fact they would have to pay the highest rate for a first time driver from a foreign country, the insurance firm had no mercy in easing the license requirement. The couple reached a decision to solve the urgent need for a driver's license by taking drivers education class, specifically designed for community adult residents at the local high school. To reduce the cost, only Yan Yun would go through the program, then, Haipin would learn from her husband.

Upon considering the couple's situation of having to walk to class, a friend of Yan Yun's classmate kindly offered Yan Yun a ride to and from the class. The program ended with the passing of a written test in school. However, the road test must be given by a state government agency. Yan Yun failed the test a couple of times on the parallel parking item. The day before he got a 30 day official temporary driver's license, ironically, Yan Yun was welcomed with a traffic ticket, issued by the local police department for parking his car on the public street in one spot all the time, in front of his apartment, and for not driving it for 30 days. Yan Yun, the financially poor student had to pay a fine for parking his own car in front of his apartment. With the temporary license Yan Yun could move his car form one spot to another. This was his first experience in driving a car.

Haipin would sit beside Yan Yun while he drove around, either shopping or weekend outdoor recreation. During the first six months after Yan Yun got his license, Haipin worried more about his driving skills than enjoying sitting in the comfortable car. His enthusiasm to drive the car surely would motivate him to use the car more often and decrease the possibility of having trouble.

The first weekend after Yan Yun got his temporary license, he took Haipin with him for a short trip to visit the rose garden, the city's showcase of beautiful flowers. This was the husband's first time to drive a five-mile trip without instructor supervision. Half way to the garden, at a curve in a narrow country road, while Yan Yun attempted to avoid hitting a parked car along the roadside, he lost control of the vehicle and hit the parked car. Unfortunately, Yun's apology to the car owner did not avoid the liability payment.

On a shopping errand to buy groceries, Haipin was shocked when Yan Yun missed a serious accident when following a car at a four-way stop sign. Haipin had a nightmare about this incident that night, and did not have peace of mind for several days.

Another time, Yan Yun was not able to avoid an accident, damaging a car driven by an elderly woman who crossed the street from a stop sign. Haipin did not know why the traffic officer still gave him a ticket for careless driving. Yan Yun had the right of way.

All of these disappointing incidents happened within six months since Yan Yun got his driver's license. The insurance company was reluctant to pay liability payments in such a short period, and they canceled the young couple's auto policy. Haipin and Yan Yun did not realize that other insurance companies in town would not consider their application for new protection unless they were willing to pay very high premiums. Since it was illegal to drive a car without liability insurance, the couple did not have any other choice but to accept the high rate offered by the company.

As Yan Yun's driving experience advanced, so did his ability to control the vehicle. He was accident free for a while. The young couple finally had family transportation that allowed them to arrive on time to school and to work as well.

This kind of expectation of being on time was sometimes badly hindered by the unpredicted mechanical malfunction of the car. Yan Yun, in order to avoid tardiness for school and work, would start the engine thirty minutes early so that he could walk instead of drive in case his car broke down.

The young couple had nothing but bad experience in owning a used car. They could not control the repair spending. One time the electrical system could not generate electricity from the battery. The repair shops could not find the real problem. They advised Yan Yun to replace the old battery with a new one. Each new battery would work only a few days. The young couple was so frustrated that they considered not owning a car. During the desperation, Yan Yun, the auto mechanic layman, decided to do one more trial before giving up. He asked the mechanic to replace the old cables with new ones. Since then the battery kept functioning. The young couple finally released the tension of tardiness for classes and for work because of car trouble. Haipin began to feel the sweet advantage of having a car.

Meanwhile, she was aware that for a one-car family she must be able to share the driving. The most convenient and economic way to learn how to operate the car was to practice with her husband. The advantage was to avoid committing time and payment for the lessons. Haipin was very enthusiastic to start this seemingly useful and fun project. To get a driver's license she must pass a written test. Haipin was worried about her ability to understand the driver's manual. She was very nervous while taking the test. When the examiner reported her score and announced that she had passed the test, she could see that her hard work paid off in preparing for the test. Furthermore, she proved that a woman could learn to drive a car just as good as a man. She was proud of her first year record that was without an accident or traffic ticket. The next adventure in her new life in the United States was to seek employment.

FIVE

Opportunity and Choice

Chapter Five

The First Job

Haipin was eagerly searching for a job, and was looking forward to settling down in the college town with her husband. She wished she could find a job as soon as possible to support the family and keep herself busy as well. However, there were many things she could not control. Unless she could ride a bus, be in a car pool, or own a car, there was simply no way she could work outside the home.

Now she had a family car and a license to operate the vehicle. The outlook for work outside the home was better than before. Though her husband used the car most of the time for daily transportation, such as attending classes at the college and going to work at his outside campus employment, Haipin could still arrange a time and a route where they could share the car.

Looking back on her years of teaching school in Manila and Taipei, Haipin never had difficulty finding a job she wanted. Human resources in her hometown was a great help. In Taipei, she got assistance from former college teachers, as well as the government bureaucracy. Certainly, Yan Yun was the major supporter in her search for new employment.

Here in the United States it was an entirely new environment. Haipin was aware that her educational background and teaching experience in Filipino and Chinese cultures would not be beneficial in allowing her to stay in her trained field. It seemed that some jobs required significant skills, and some required muscles. Thus, she began her adventure in searching for employment opportunities in the non-skilled labor market.

Haipin set her employment goal in the field of general help or assembly-line work. It was not her best choice, but she had no relatives or friends who might help her as she had before coming to America. Now it was time for her to learn, to work, and to survive in a land of opportunities.

First, she contacted retail stores in person for job vacancies. She did the same at nearby manufacturing plants. From these contacts she learned that the easy way to land a job was not going door to door, but to register with the government employment agency. She found out that a local office of the state of Missouri employment service center was in walking distance from her apartment.

Employees of the local state employment agency were nice, nicer than Haipin expected from government bureaucrats and those she encountered in Manila and Taipei. The counselor was patiently listening to her background briefing, occasionally smiling at her while she searched for a proper word from her English vocabulary.

Upon registering with the agency, Haipin immediately received a vacancy list of job openings. In some cases, the employment counselor called the employer for current status. Jobs available at that point were babysitters, housekeepers, janitors, and manufacturing production workers. After consideration of advantages on location and wages, Haipin chose one as an operator at the assembly line with UMCO Fishing Equipment, a fishing pole and fishing related products company in suburban Cape Girardeau, about five miles from her residence. She could report to work the coming Monday. The employment service was so helpful that Haipin called it a 'one stop' service. She was excited, believing in the greatness of the United States, a democratic society and land of opportunities, with a purpose of serving the people.

Haipin and her husband worked out a schedule to perfectly fit both of them, sharing the family car to and from college classes, as well as their work. Imagine the good feeling for the young couple in having two paychecks each week! Since Haipin worked a full-time job, she made more money than her student husband, though her hourly wage was one dollar and twenty cents.

The Working Class

As a trained teaching professional who had been in the teaching field for several years, Haipin had to adjust her thinking and life style in order to meet the big change. The transition from a creative minded academic person to a muscle-oriented working class was not easy. Looking back to her childhood, the spoiled mid class family's daughter, never thought she might make a living using her muscles.

In order to survive for her husband's education and her support role as a student wife in a new land, Haipin determined to accept the reality that a low paying, unskilled job was her way of making a living. In the United States, her career would be in working class through her employment history, regardless of the change in status of her husband.

Haipin's desire for work made her current working class job less relevant to what she previously did for employment. She did not care what kind of a job, but valued the opportunity to have a job and continued doing it happily. This was the fundamental philosophy that Haipin held since she began her first paid employment after completing her college program in the Philippines.

The kind of work-oriented enthusiastic attitudes had continued as Haipin began her production work on the assembly line at the UMCO. She was not nervous when she entered the corporate building. The security guard pointed her to the personnel office to file employment papers. The foreman had already been there to assist her in completing hiring procedures. After signing several documents, which she never had time to read, and tried to understand, she walked out of the office, with the foreman bringing her an employee ID and time card. She first needed to learn how to punch-in and punch-out the time card. As the foreman gave her a tour of the cafeteria, the employee's locker room, and the do's and don'ts policy, she was convinced that every profession had something to learn, including an unskilled labor worker.

The building tour ended with the entering of the main production floor. Haipin punched her time card and walked into the production hall. The noise from operating machinery made it difficult to communicate with the foreman and co-workers. The machines kept everyone busy. Only a few workers noticed the new employee's presence. The foreman then introduced Haipin to the line leader that would give instruction and operation detail on the part of the product for which she would be held responsible.

It was really a big change, as compared to her first day in teaching at an elementary school. Here Haipin minded only the part of the product she worked on. She was eager to introduce herself to co-workers next to her station on the same line, however, workers were not allowed to chat with one another. In fact, no one could hear anything, other than the loud noise from the operating machinery. There was no such social activity as a 'welcome new employee party' as she had experienced in her previous employment.

On the job, she was told to raise her hand in case she needed supplies or problems arose, but avoid stopping the continuous process as the product passed through her station. In any situation, the line leader, the foreman, or standby worker would come to her assistance immediately upon seeing her raised hand. The same procedure was applied to anyone on the production line who needed to go to the restroom. These procedures reminded her of a similar policy required by her students when going out of the classroom to the restroom, or to see the principal while classes were in session to get permission from the teacher. She still had the past experience in her mind.

Though the job did not require much muscle strength, it did require attention all the time. A mistake on one station might cause the entire production line to slow down. Haipin took her job seriously. She had more education than the rest of the workers at the production unit. She would feel bad if she made a mistake.

On the production line, time, quality, and quantity went side by side. Any of the three, if not perfectly matched, could increase the cost of production, and thus lower the profit margin for the employer because of the huge returns. As a professional trained young woman, Haipin never thought it was a problem to meet this goal, regardless of whether it was in the field of teaching as she once did, or manufacturing that she was currently doing.

If there were something she was not quite comfortable with on the job in the early part of her employment, it would be trying to match speed with the machine while installing the product pieces together. Like other co-workers, Haipin was allowed to take a 15-minute break for every two hours of work. Besides sore muscles in her arms, standing all the time at the workstation made her legs sore as well. As time went by, and at the end of three months' probation period, she passed the quantity and quality requirements. Her physical strength increased as well.

It was a phenomenon she never experienced before, break time. As the bell sounded to start a break, a dash began. Many of her assembly line co-workers wasted no time in competing with high speed for limited seating space available at the cafeteria. Others ran to get a chance to use the restroom. For smokers, at that time, the chance to use the restroom was so nice. They could enjoy smoking and relieve their urgency with ease.

Haipin had learned for the fist time in industrialized America, that the relationship between laborers and management was serious. Contracting agreement rules, rather than giving the human side consideration was the practice. Workers must be at his/her station on time. Five to ten minutes late would constitute being tardy. Any worker receiving three tardy notices would be dismissed from employment. A tardy would be counted as half an hour absence when figuring hourly earnings.

On the other side of the coin, the labor union saw to it that every worker who was a member of the organization would not work even a few minutes longer than the specified time. The worker would stop production and leave his/her station immediately, regardless if it only took a few seconds additional time to complete a job. The worker would ask for overtime pay for any additional time for any work over five minutes.

However, the seemingly no compromise stand between the two sides, the management and the labor, could work harmoniously on some social and human side events. The employer could sponsor birthday parties; Thanksgiving, Christmas, and New Year's Day celebrations for the workers. Some workers might get bonus pay for their work being well done.

In return, the workers would volunteer their time for promoting a good image of the employer in such community service programs as raising funds for charities, public health awareness, etc.

As time went by, Haipin began to understand how the management and labor production teams worked. Either side had their interests and concerns to be addressed. However, all sides could work together for common benefits. In the oriental society, people talked about loyalty. Loyalty became a good behavior for an employee. No worker would think his/her rights were violated. Therefore Haipin, being a production line worker, praised the system that provided workers the opportunity to express their concerns.

Surprisingly, Haipin never expected that she could be well received by the management and co-workers as well. She did not have production experience in a manufacturing setting, her muscles that were required to do the job were not strong, and her verbal communication might be a little unclear for the main stream English speaking work force at the plant.

Happy Learning

Her humble self-assessment helped her pursue a better perspective by working hard on the job, as well as inter personal relations. She understood that she was unique, in that she was a foreign worker in the workforce and she would not be treated as a guest much longer.

A big challenge to her in surviving the new job, was the eight-hour period of standing at her workstation. Physically she was sore all over. Rationally it was her investment for making a living. Haipin recognized that nothing was so sweet as a short break, so her legs could enjoy a few minutes of relaxation. She wished she could win the race for a vacant seat in the cafeteria when the break bell sounded.

Nature makes sense; Haipin's muscles got stronger day by day. It was good to feel the uncomfortable feeling slowly disappear. The three months probation period had just passed. She received a strong recommendation for her job performance. Haipin now had the level of energy needed to do the job. The sore muscles had gone. Now she focused on the production, quantity with quality.

It was a new, but better feeling when she received her weekly paycheck. The foreman delivered it to her in person at her workstation after the last break on Friday. She still remembered the once a month salary in an envelope while teaching school in Taipei. Instead of feeling in good spirits each month, she had a good feeling four times within the same period. Wow! It was in U.S. dollars, the most stable currency in the world.

It was even a better feeling when Haipin's husband brought home a paycheck every Friday from his off campus part-time employment. The young couple could set aside a portion of their earnings in a bank savings account.

Haipin was pleased that she had an opportunity to learn things from her trained professional field. She had learned from her current job as an assembly line operator that the job itself would not discriminate against anyone committed to doing the job well. Only the mind of a person weighing the opportunity matters.

The young couple's first step in living in the United States apparently had built a beachhead. Haipin did not mind that she was a manufacturing production worker, and was still a student wife. She thought positively. She could do a good job in her employment, she could make contributions to the family income to help support her husband's education, and most of all, she was very happy.

SIX

Life in the Riverside Town

Chapter Six

The River, The Rose Garden, The Campus, The Conveyer Belt, and The House Wife

Haipin had lived with her husband in a little house in Cape Girardeau since she first arrived in the United States in May 1968. In her early days in elementary school, she was fascinated with the legendary Mississippi River. Yes, there are many stories about the background of the river. Haipin remembered telling Mark Twain's *The Adventures of Huckleberry Finn* to the children in her fourth grade class in Taiwan.

How nice to have a chance to see in person the vessels carrying tourists, or loaded with cargo, cruising down the mighty waterway. There are also fishing fans spending their leisure time on the river shore. Haipin was excited over the fact that her residence was just a couple of miles from the waterfront. The couple sometimes simply took a walk to the river resort for a break from their busy work schedule. Occasionally, they drove across the bridge to tour villages on the Illinois side of the river on Highway 3.

Haipin began to take life easier in the river front town. Though she and Yan Yun did not have many friends, and thus did not attend many social activities, they found they could have fun without going to parties or out-of-town trips. In addition to the big river, they could easily access the city's rose gardens, the beautiful college campus, and the picturesque residences.

The residence the young couple shared with the house owner was located at the foot of a hill, a short walking distance from the main college campus. Large trees lined both sides of the street, making good shade. Haipin considered the short streets around her house as beautiful trails in a botanic garden. All neighboring houses had well maintained lawns. The boundary that separated each household was bushes or flowering trees, rather than high wooden fences. Neighbors could wave their hands to greet the next door neighbors, while strolling or working in the backyard. Haipin's next door neighbor was a group of college students. In the summer time, as the temperature reached 90 degrees Fahrenheit, the students would lie on the lawn for a sunbath. Haipin could not believe her eyes, seeing that her husband was still interested in peeping at girls at the next door lawn.

Lonely in A Hustle Bustle Life

Though Haipin lived with her husband going into the fourth honeymoon year, socially she felt lonely. She thought in time, that interpersonal relations, such as meeting people and making new friends might help. The hustle and bustle of daily life did occupy most her time, but she could not help but miss the warmness of friendship with others, that could be found in social activities.

She first thought of searching for friends with a similar culture background. Unfortunately, no community sources led to the discovery of folks from China, the Philippines or Taiwan. The local college did have a small international students club, but none of its members came from the Chinese culture.

One day Haipin was excited when Yan Yun brought good news from the college. Two faculty members, Dr. Wu, who taught physics and Mr. Huang, who taught political science, both from Taiwan, started teaching at the current semester when Yan Yun enrolled as a new graduate student. The two professors' spouses were also Chinese from Taiwan. Later, a Chinese woman, with her Caucasian husband, who was a member of the college teaching faculty, joined the small social activity group. Haipin and her husband thus became active members of the club. In addition to celebrating American festivals, they also enjoyed sharing the joyous spirits of Chinese New Year Day, Lantern Day, and Autumn Festival. As time went by, the young couple no longer felt homesick. The loneliness had gone; a new feeling of multi-cultural society began to emerge.

The Routine Extra

As the production process on the assembly line became routine, and her muscles began to adjust to this particular job, Haipin found that assembling fishing poles, though boring, was, at least a job. Any job is worthy of being done well. She believed that fishing fans that chose to use poles of her workmanship would appreciate her and say 'job well done.' She enjoyed doing this kind of boring, yet easy job. She enjoyed not having to spend time on lesson plans, as she did while teaching school.

Haipin considered working overtime as recognition of a worker's good job, a reward for someone's accomplishment. She always welcomed overtime work, and knew the assignments well. All of her supervisors knew they could count on her when overtime work was needed, especially on holidays.

Her overtime work on the assembly line did not interfere with her assuming the student's wife duty. Typing book reports and research papers for her husband's college assignments became another routine extra. It was a new experience, just like she learned processing fishing poles at the production line station. Any item that was not properly done at any individual's station would not pass through the quality control system. Any misspelling of a word, or not using capital letters properly on a college research paper would be returned and receive a bad grade.

Haipin took a typing class in high school. However, she had only basic skills. The typing of a college paper is a serious task. The professor or teaching assistant, who evaluates the paper, has been trained to find mistakes. This was something a student wished to avoid. Haipin tried, to the best of her ability to avoid mistakes in her typing, thus helping her husband receive a better grade on his assignment.

The history of Haipin's routine extra jobs in typing started as early as the first week she lived with her husband in the college town. It was prior to her paid job with the fishing pole manufacturing company. Writing book reports and research papers apparently is a major part of student's assignment in American colleges. Her husband's graduate program required even more paper work.

Since Yan Yun's typing was awful, it was a headache for him to even think of the writing assignment. The last two semesters in college before Haipin came, he paid for typing by spending hard earned, below minimum wage dollars from part-time, off campus employment. Haipin, though not an expert typist, accepted the typing work willingly, as part of her support of her husband's college education.

Typing assignments, though not an every day requirement, had to be completed by Haipin by the required due date. Since Yan Yun was in a graduate program, every course required at least one major paper each semester.

The hustle and bustle of academic typing began by having to use a typewriter. The poor student family did not think they could afford a new typewriter in the first place. The only thing they could think of was to use the free typing lab facility. However, this free service was still not a good choice. Because of the limited time that the facility was open to the students, it was difficult for

Haipin, the full-time assembly line worker and student wife, to make the best use of her available time. Meanwhile, the pressure on her to meet the deadline for turning in academic papers was tremendous.

Out of the frustration of typing papers, Haipin made a bold decision to own a typewriter. Since typing a paper was an important part of academic work, there was no reason why she should not own a typewriter. She considered owning a typewriter for doing academic assignments was as necessary as owning a car for earning necessary employment.

Though the used a heavy-duty manual typewriter, an Olivetti Underwood 21, it was expensive (equal to one week take-home pay), Haipin was excited that she could best use her available time working at home. She was tired of walking to and from the college library and trying to memorize the typing room's open and close time schedule. Since then, the typewriter became another partner in sharing her family life, other than her husband.

Typing a college paper was in no way considered an easy job. The correction method at that time was to use correction liquid, which could look bad, especially if it covered many words on the page. The time spent on the correction process was less productive and led to feelings of frustration. The author, her husband, was indecisive in the use of the vocabulary, which increased the frequency of encountering errors.

The big challenge to the student wife was typing a major research paper, a thesis for Master of Arts degree. For some reason, Yan Yun chose to write a thesis instead of taking a comprehensive general examination, as most of his classmates did.

This reason, as explained by her husband, was simple. Yan Yun did not have confidence in passing the comprehensive examination. He, however, did believe strongly that he could complete the theses within a year. In any situation, if you have an alternative choice, you should choose the better one. He realized that the typing task for this major academic research paper would add a tremendous burden on Haipin. Thus, he asked her for understanding and support.

The pressure for completion of the thesis was high. The young couple wished to get out their student and minimum wage labor life as soon as possible. Yan Yun, upon receiving a Master of Arts degree, would start a career with a better future. He planned to graduate a year after completing thirty-three credit hours of coursework. Within this plan, the draft copy of the thesis must be turned in to his major advisor in the fall semester, with the approved copy two months before the end of spring semester. Then Yan Yun could receive the diploma at the university commencement in the summer.

The hustle and bustle of typing work began slowly, and increased as the date approached the submission deadline. The concern was not how fast Haipin could type. She could finish typing the five-chapter thesis in a couple of weeks with her available time. However, the frequent re-writings and changes on the paper made the typing a boring task.

It is hard for a non-English speaking native to have confidence in using the English vocabulary. Yan Yun was not comfortable using certain words in his paper. Replacing a single word on the draft could require Haipin to type a new page or pages.

The typing of her husband's thesis was a headache for the student wife. Haipin was tired of working on the same chapter again and again. Yan Yun was advised to send a very rough copy of a chapter to his academic advisor each time. When the paper was returned from the advisor with comments, corrections, omissions, additions, Yan Yun could spend weeks re-writing and re-organizing the paper. Haipin would work on the typewriter days and nights on the draft copy. After the new draft copy reached the advisor, another corrected copy was returned for rework. She hated to see the pages of her work thrown into the trash basket. At times Haipin became frustrated, but was eager to see the final draft copy.

Yan Yun turned in the final good copy to the graduate school in time. The completion of a timely task made Haipin cheer up and be proud of her accomplishment. Her high spirits did not last long, as the graduate school returned the paper to Yan Yun for rework on the correction liquid covered words. Because the approved good copy would be included in the library's permanent collection, the graduate school would not accept a thesis with corrected words beyond its requirements. The deadline for turning in was a week prior to graduation. Yan Yun would not be allowed to get the diploma until the approved thesis was on file at the graduate school.

Haipin had to ask for a one week leave from her employer to work on the typing. The final good copy should include one copy on 20-pound paper and three on onionskin paper on one typing. The hard part was that no liquid corrected word could be accepted. This was a tremendous pressure on her to avoid typing errors. Since there was no way she could do perfect typing, she had to prepare herself for working a long time on each page. The most disappointing work was in finding only a single mistake in an entire finished page. Working on a re-done page was not a pleasant task for a student wife who was proud of her work. The time spent on repeat work, the money wasted on typing supplies (paper goes to the wastebasket), and the wages lost from her absence at the production line with her employer were things Haipin most regretted. However, as the college accepted the final good copy of her husband's thesis, she was cheered up for her contributions to the last touch of Yan Yun's academic program at Southeast Missouri State College.

On the thirty-first of May, 1970, at the 96th commencement ceremony, Haipin was excited to witness her husband's accomplishment, the earning of a Master of Arts degree. She was proud to be a student wife at the ceremony when Yan Yun received his Bachelor of Arts at Tamkang College of Arts and Sciences in Taipei, 1965. Here again Haipin was proud to be a student wife while her husband received his Master of Arts degree. .

Innocent /Guilty

Since Haipin came to live with her husband in the college town, the young couple seemed to have their minds filled with nothing but hard work on academic projects and production line wage earnings. At this current financial status, they did not have a plan to change the family structure by having a baby. Haipin wished to put this option on hold until they started a good career.

At a routine check up with her family physician, Haipin was surprised by the news that she was pregnant. This required the young couple to take proper action immediately. Some of the actions would involve Haipin's full time employment. There was no part-time worker or leave without pay policy offered by the employer at that time. Judging from her current energy level and good health, Haipin decided to hold the full time job for a while, but would stop working at the advice of her physician.

To become a mother is a woman's natural phenomenon, fostering her love to another generation. Haipin was excited over it, however, she could not keep from thinking of the financial hardship. How could her husband pay family bills as well as his college expenses? Yan Yun could only work part-time. The dilemma had been lingering with her for months. Haipin still had a feeling of guilt over her first miscarriage, while working as a full-time schoolteacher in Taiwan.

With the professional advice from her family physician, Haipin was confident she could work at her usual level on the production line with UMCO Fishing Equipment Company, at least for another three months. She was not bothered from standing all the time at work; since she had been doing this for a year. She never slowed down her pace of productivity as the months of her pregnancy advanced. Her supervisor or co-workers did not know she was pregnant.

Her confidence in continuing to work for three more months was beginning to weaken as she experienced increasing discomfort at work. One day during her first month of pregnancy, she suddenly rushed to the restroom where she lost the fetus. Compared to her previous miscarriage, this was just a minor pain. Fortunately, it happened about one hour before time to get off work. She would keep this incident confidential. Instead of going home, Yan Yun drove her directly to the nearby hospital. Haipin was so happy that no serious complications were found during the check up at the emergency room. She did not consider resting at home for a couple of days. Haipin, as usual reported to her job at the UMCO the next day, treating the incident as if nothing happened.

Under such difficult financial circumstances, they did not know how they would be able to add a new member to the family. The young couple did not make plans as to when they would have a child. Yan Yun was not much interested in having a baby until he started a career. However Haipin took a neutral position. She did not plan to have a baby, but neither did she wish to terminate a pregnancy. Though she was innocent on this issue, Haipin felt a little guilt for losing two babies due to miscarriages. She began to have another thought.

Although Haipin was still in child bearing years, the feeling of 'the clock ticking' made her think of having children just as important as having her job. She wondered if she could have saved the two pregnancies if she had chosen to slow down her regular activity. She could make money in a future career, but time was not on her side for raising children.

When Haipin got pregnant again, she wasted no time in submitting her resignation to her employer, the UMCO Fishing Equipment Company. It was a coincidence, that after completion of his MA degree, Yan Yun planned to move out of the college town for a new adventure of job searching, or getting into a further education program. There was no need for Haipin to keep her employment. For the time being, she had the time to take a break from a busy work schedule and take care of the pregnancy.

On the eve of leaving the college town, Haipin had mixed feelings about memories of living in the riverside community. Three years' residence in a place is not really a long period, though it was the longest one since she and her husband moved there from their home countries in Asia.

Haipin was excited about everything in America. Probably the first thing that impressed her was the hospitality of friendly people. While she and her husband went to the grocery store on foot, very often they were invited to ride with a driver they had never met. Though sort of homesick, Haipin kept herself busy, and tried hard to adjust to life in the local community. She had a burning enthusiasm to learn. In order to improve speaking the English language, she bought a pre-owned 13-inch black and white television set as a learning tool. To become a licensed driver of a car was something she never dreamed would happen. She adjusted well to work in a manufacturing environment. She helped her husband complete typing a major research paper, a thesis for the MA degree. She was proud to be a student wife. If there was anything she regretted, it was her miscarriages. Now she was pregnant again and was about to leave the community. With great expectation, Haipin wished this baby would be a great personality and a great achiever; one that a mother could be proud. She would consider it a priceless present made in this community.

The *'Long March'*

Moving out of the Cape Girardeau community did not mean a lot of changes for the young couple. Yan Yun's graduate degree from Southeast Missouri State College did not land him a professional job. He planned to be a student again for another graduate degree. Thus Haipin would remain a student wife.

Yan Yun had planned to attend the summer school at the University of Oklahoma at Norman. Then he would start an MSL degree program at Emporia State College in Kansas in the fall. The couple packed all their belongings in their 8-year old, small 1962 Buick sedan. Household property items considered valuable were a 13-inch black and white television set, the Olivetti Underwood manual typewriter, and the Taiwan made electric rice cooker.

Haipin looked at the 600 mile one way trip as an adventure. They would take US 60 west, then Interstate 44 south. Some uncertain things lingered in their minds. It was Yan Yun's debut of driving long hours through mountain routes on high speed Interstate Highways. Anything could happen, since their only driving experience had been on streets where the speed limit was only 35 miles an hour. Neither Yan Yun or Haipin had much knowledge about the mechanics in handling auto emergencies. The couple was well aware that the eight-year old used car had already experienced several breakdowns.

Here Haipin faced another problem. Her physical condition of a three-month pregnancy needed special care. Not only could she not take turns in driving, she also needed frequent restroom stops, ranging from 30 minutes to one-hour. In fact, there were not many roadside stops available. In order to survive the urgent needs, Haipin utilized any empty container available for purchase at roadside stores so it could serve the function of collecting urine in the car. Haipin never anticipated such embarrassing moments while traveling on the road. Yan Yun would stop at the roadside anywhere and anytime by her request so she could do whatever was needed to make her feel more comfortable. She could not imagine how bad the situation would be if her husband was not a caring person.

In order not to give her husband too much pressure by her demands, Haipin let Yan Yun totally control the driving as well as the choosing of a motel. He would like to avoid rush hours while traveling in the city, or he would get nervous, which could result in loosing control of the vehicle. He preferred to stay in a motel out of the city limits, for low rent price and less traffic congestion.

At about three o'clock one afternoon on a dry hot summer day (June 4, 1970), without warning, a sudden storm popped up as the couple's car traveled through the metro area of Springfield, Missouri. The city was under a heavy storm, with visibility of about five miles. Yan Yun was extremely nervous. He wished to find a shelter nearby on the freeway, but he lost directions in a new city. In such an emergency situation, Haipin could not help but urged her husband to keep calm. She silently prayed for the safety of the family; her husband, herself, and the unborn baby.

Yan Yun tried hard to manage several lane changes in the heavy traffic on the freeway, and parked his car on the shoulder provided for emergency stops. The strong storm with lightning lasted more than an hour. The couple could do nothing but close their eyes and pray for nature's mercy.

The storm did not change Yan Yun's preference for a motel outside the city limits. As the rain was over and sunset light reappeared in the remote sky horizon, Haipin suggested checking into a motel at the next exit. However, the still energetic husband insisted on driving an hour or so for lodging. Yan Yun drove past hotels with 'no vacancy' signs one after another. It was getting dark. Haipin worried they might be driving all night and still not find a vacancy. She wished that a man could understand more about how uncomfortable it was for a pregnant woman, buckled in the seat of a car for long travel. Yan Yun, however, blamed his poor driving skills, along with indecisive action that would prepare well for an exit.

The pressure of the sky getting dark made Yan Yun decide against his preference for a motel out of the city limits. They finally exited to the City of Mt. Vernon, about 60 miles southwest of Springfield on Interstate 44. This was the couple's first motel experience at Motel Cortel for a double bed at $8.24. Considering less than one-dollar take-home pay per hour for Haipin and much less for Yan Yun, this amount could be considered luxury spending.

Haipin had too much on her mind; the uncertainty of her husband's summer school, his further studies at Emporia State College, the job opportunity after graduation, the lack of a stable family income, and the expenses and care of the coming newborn baby.

Thanks to their hard working days in Cape Girardeau, they did build a minimum safety fund for survival living on the campus for a semester or so. During the last three years the couple did keep a savings account in the bank. They brought with them a check of $2,500 after closing the account.

Though there was little base for optimism, Haipin and her husband looked for a miracle as compared to the Chinese Communists *'long march'*. The term *'long march'* has been known in the 20th century Chinese history since the founding of the People's Republic of China in 1949. The Chinese Communists' People's Liberation Army regained strength from her 2500 *Li* retreat to Yen An, avoiding total defeat and later won the Civil War. Haipin and her husband symbolized their leaving Cape Girardeau, to Norman, Oklahoma, 600 miles of driving as a *'long march.'*

'Thank God, we are safe and sound!' The couple finally cheered up as their *'long march'* reached its destiny at the University town of Norman, Oklahoma without a problem the next day. They immediately unloaded their car and moved in a reserved married students apartment.

Sharing: A Small World of International Community

Living in the married student housing, Haipin became a full-time student wife to support her full-time student husband. She slowly gained weight as her pregnancy progressed toward maturity. Though she was not allowed to work, Haipin kept herself busy doing house chores such as cooking, laundry, typing her husband's college assignment papers, and checking up on her physical changes as required by her physician.

The apartment unit was very special. Many married couples came from foreign countries. Haipin enjoyed a good friendship with the next door neighbors. It was a good opportunity to learn and share cultural heritage and customs with apartment neighbors who were natives of that culture. One of her next door neighbors was an American Caucasian from another state. She was a single mother with three school age kids. Haipin admired her ability to take care of kids, work part-time, and at the same time, take classes at the university. Though Haipin was sorry to hear of the single mom's unhappy stories of three marriages, she was moved by the young mother's strong determination to pursue a better education, leading to brighter future.

In this apartment compound, Haipin got acquainted with several student wives who were in a situation similar to hers; pregnant and a full-time housewife. Though each one had their own native language, all of them spoke English and shared common interests, such as pregnancy, caring for the baby and raising a child. The popular culture exchange was food and cooking. For Haipin's contribution, the egg roll was a favorite food and received good applause. Sharing common interests made Haipin's daily life easier.

Haipin was impressed by the fast pace the kids learned to speak languages other than their mother tongue. Little kids in the apartment spoke their mother tongue at home. It was amazing that some kids not yet in school, while playing outside the home, could communicate with one another in English.

Being a school teacher before coming to the United States, Haipin was very much interested in observing how pre-school kids, with different native languages could play together without learning a common language, that is, the spoken English. She did notice some beginner English speakers had an accent and broken sentences. Somehow the natural instinct might play a role for their mutual understanding. The apartment playground thus becomes a self-paced learning ground. Haipin concluded that the big English speaking environment of adult conversation, television, and radio, might play a major roll in the success of kids' language skills.

As summer school was over, the couple packed and continued on a journey north. Yan Yun would start a new academic year with a new Master's degree program at Emporia State College in Kansas. Haipin would keep her student wife status, but with a new lookout for an additional role as a mother when her newborn baby was due. Another challenge was ahead.

SEVEN

Amid the Prairies

Chapter Seven

Northward to the Heart Land

Yan Yun was glad that he earned six credit hours in the summer at the cost of $300 tuition, plus $900 food and housing. Half of their savings was gone.

The couple packed and continued their adventurous trip north. This was their second relocation in mid-land America since leaving Cape Girardeau, Missouri. This time they would move north from Oklahoma to Kansas, the geographic center of the continental (48 states) U.S.A.

Kansas is amidst the great prairies of the American agricultural zone, and a state with vast plains, and a panoramic landscape of rolling hills. Yan Yun planned to live here for further education, as well as possibly landing a career. Haipin thus remained a supportive spouse, a student wife, working as much as she could.

The destination of this move was Emporia, a college town where Emporia State College is located. On this relocation trip, Yan Yun was not as nervous as his first 600-mile trip from Cape Girardeau, Missouri to Norman, Oklahoma. However, the odds for the car breaking down on the busy Interstate highway was on his mind. Another concern would be Haipin's fatigue, due to her pregnancy.

The couple had their car inspected for safe driving. Most of the vital parts of the vehicle, as recommended by an auto repair mechanic, had been fixed prior to the trip. Though Haipin did not believe that the 245 mile trip required replacing four tires, the couple did pay for this new part just to feel safe.

It was 100 degrees Fahrenheit, on a hot summer day, August 26, 1970. Haipin was in good sprits, and looked forward to seeing a new place with new opportunities and the hope of prosperity ahead, as a result of their hard work and determination.

The 8-year old used Chevrolet sedan, loaded with all of their household belongings seemed to be functioning smoothly at the beginning, and as it continued traveling north on the Interstate 35. Haipin would take a break at roadside service stations as often as needed in order to reduce the uncomfortable feeling of being buckled in the seat. She, after two miscarriages, took seriously the safety of her pregnancy this time.

In a good mood, the couple had the hot weather and fatigue temporarily out of mind, and, instead talked about how to care for the baby; the feeding, the bathing, the crying at midnight.... Then, the daycare, the kindergarten...

Haipin was so excited to learn that Emporia, the destination of the trip was just 30 something miles away, as the couple left the last service station in the toll route section. It was about two o'clock in the afternoon and hot and humid. Though the air-conditioning system still worked, the quality of cool air was getting weak. The couple was aware that something might be wrong while climbing up a hill. First the car moved forward at a very slow speed against the gas pedal, then suddenly, the accelerator was dead. The car stopped half way on an uphill highway. At the same time, smoke came from beneath the hood. The couple got out of the smoking car immediately. Haipin was scared and did not know how long she might have to suffer. Yan Yun had trouble keeping his calm too. He stood at the shoulder and cried for help.

Thank God, a passing car stopped at the scene and the driver helped extinguish the fire. He found that the leaking water caused the heat to build on the engine. Yan Yun could not understand why the auto repair people did not do a good job on the radiator. They put the safety of the poor student family in jeopardy.

Haipin and her husband were offered a ride with the driver to a nearby service station. There, the good-hearted helpful driver explained the emergency to the station manger, which called for a towing service. Both Yan Yun and Haipin lacked this sort of experience in handling auto breakdowns on a busy highway. It was frustrating and depressed the couple to try to accomplish anything because of their language barrier at that time. The car breakdown could have been worse, had it not been for the great help given by the nice man. Haipin felt guilty that she did not retain his name.

The couple was seated beside the driver in the tow truck for the rest of the trip. Haipin had mixed feelings as she turned her head back and looked at the disabled sedan on the deck of the truck. It was lucky there was no one hurt, or no damage to the engine from fire. However, the cost to purchase another vehicle was too expensive for the unemployed couple. In addition, funds were needed for the hospital bill when Haipin gave birth to their child soon. Worries could not solve problems; the couple believed they could work toward a better future with their determination to be successful.

The wrecker service truck took them and the disabled car to an auto repair shop upon arrival in Emporia, Kansas. At this point, the couple lost the advantage of driving around, going whenever or wherever they wished. They were very tired. Haipin was eager to move in the apartment they rented. The problem was not that easy to solve. Unless they wished to pay for a rental car and unload cargo from the disabled car, they would not be able to cook or lie on the bed. Their budget for spending more was extremely tight.

The couple could not do anything other than patiently wait for the damage assessment and the shop's recommendation. Under the 100-degree hot weather, the two frustrated travelers realized that they did not have many options. They must accept the lowest price offer available.

Here was the shop's assessment on the disabled car. Unless a new or a functional used engine replaced the old one, the 8 year, 80,000 miles Chevrolet sedan would be disabled for good and would go to the junkyard.

The lowest price for a used engine, the repairman said, would be $400. The total repair payment, including engine and labor, was $500. A warranty of one year on the engine and three months for workmanship would be given. Or, the shop manger said, he could sell them a good used car for a discount price.

The couple's patience was at its end. Yan Yun decided to buy a used car at $500, or a little more, instead of spending $400 on a troubled used car with a rebuilt engine. Haipin believed it was a good practical decision under current circumstances.

What surprised the young couple was the auto shop management's willingness to help a customer, as well as their competence and efficiency in handling the business transaction. Upon knowing the couple's intention to buy a used car, the manager offered help in financing the purchase. 'To do business with a graduate student who has a family is a sound practice' he said. Yan Yun did confirm to the auto shop dealer his employment with Iowa Beef, a large beef processor, and one of the major hiring employers in the college town.

Haipin never thought they could own a car simply by putting a signature on a bank loan paper. The couple traded in their disabled Chevrolet sedan for a 5-year old

Ford Falcon for $1,000. They paid down $50 and drove the Falcon home. They would pay the installment monthly for three years.

Haipin, now more than ever, believed that American capitalism was not as bad as was portrayed by the governments of socialist countries. American business, of course, makes money; however at the same time, they offer assistance to the customer with expectation of his satisfaction.

Yan Yun, released from the daylong frustration of car trouble, wasted no time in driving his 'new' used car home. Prior to moving into the rented house, he stopped at the personnel office of Iowa Beef. The hiring official did ask a few questions and handed him a W-2 form. Yan Yun was allowed to turn in his choice of shift and time schedule later, after his confirmation of college classes. The employment opportunity had boosted the couple's spirits and kept peace of mind in bank loan obligations.

Haipin began her new life, assuming a new role as a full-time housewife, plus status of student spouse in her third time college town residence. It was the first time that she did not have any intention of working. She had a very important role of becoming a mother. Her expectation for giving birth to a baby could be anytime in the next few months.

As a full-time housewife, Haipin did grocery shopping, cooking, laundry, and preparing her husband's lunch box. After long-time classroom teaching and assembly line production, Haipin enjoyed the peaceful home environment, at least for a while.

However, she could not totally give up the supportive role as a student wife. Yan Yun enrolled 12 semester credit hours at Emporia State College. A student who takes twelve hours graduate level credit is classified as a full-time student. Meanwhile, he worked full-time at a night shift clean up duty. Haipin wanted to lessen her husband's workload. She could work as a typist, an easy but time consuming job, typing research papers as she did while her husband worked on his Master of Arts degree.

Yan Yun's full-time employment helped the family financially and gave them a good feeling as well. Haipin was more secure, now, more than ever as she learned that Iowa Beef, her husband's employer, would extend its full-time employee's health insurance benefits to the spouse. She did not have to pay from her own pocket the hospital bill and doctor's office visits as well. Currently she enjoyed the short period of freedom from the hustle and bustle. Her priority as a mother to be and student wife was to take care of her pregnancy and to type her husband's college papers.

The Joyous Strain

From hot summer to falling leaves and chilly frosty autumn mornings, Haipin had settled down to her temporary residency in the college town of Emporia, Kansas for nearly six months. It was a period of tranquil days since she started her career. Routine chores such as cooking, laundering, typing, and regular check ups with the doctor seemed to be boring. However she thought of it in a different way. Haipin would be glad to have time for reading, a habit since she was a schoolgirl. She would enjoy watching her favorite television programs. A new subject of interest was to learn as much as possible on nursing a baby.

Haipin's residence was a one story, one bedroom small old house. She never had many chances to chat with her next door neighbor for developing a good friendship. Most of the time the single woman was not home. Thus Haipin reached out to the Toso family across the street. It worked well. For years to come, the two families became close friends. Nothing was more important than to have friends within a short walking distance. Haipin and her husband did not have relatives in the United States. Now they had close friends who would extend helping hands in time of need. The Tosoes gave Haipin a sense of security in knowing she had help as the expectation of her baby approached.

Looking back to days when she was a spoiled child, a happy college girl, and later a career woman, Haipin always enjoyed people around her. She never felt lonely.

At this time, she was alone at home most of the day. Her husband worked the evening shift at the Iowa Beef facilities, and attended classes at the college in the morning. She could not expect a regular weekend just for the two of them. Yan Yun might go to the library doing research or preparing for a test, or he could work overtime on his off campus job. The only sure time together with Yan Yun was midnight, or early morning when he returned from work. If he had an eight o'clock morning class, he would leave home at seven. These few hours together were their precious time of the day.

'The world belongs to two of us' is just romantic thinking for two individuals in love. Haipin, however, thought things beyond. Living in a foreign land without relatives and friends around, it seemed as if she was isolated on a deserted island. Even though the Tosoes might offer a helping hand it could not eliminate her fear of emergencies. Haipin's mind was filled with worries such as the safety of her husband's workplace, his driving on the busy streets and highways, and above all, the immediate attentions needed on her pregnant medical care.

At times Haipin was tormented with some symptoms that she would like to understand better, especially in recent days. She wished her mom or mother-in-law could be available for consultation. In some cases, she was in a dilemma on whether or not to visit the doctor. If so, she still needed to wait for her husband's availability. He was not home most of the time; either in school or at work. They had only one car. She could not afford to pay a taxi, should the symptoms be considered an emergency.

The high spirits of becoming a mother finally overcame Haipin's concern. She now focused on the expected day, and would enjoy holding the new baby, touching and kissing. Though the technology was not able to predict the gender of the coming baby at that time, the couple did not consider a preference in the baby's sex. What mattered most was the newborn's health. Therefore two names; one for a boy, the other for a girl were chosen.

Yan Yun, the father-to-be would pick a name for a boy. If it were a girl, Haipin would name the newborn child. The couple came to a final vote from a list of names: Ray for a boy, and Serene for a girl. Ray, in a physics phenomenon, is a beam of radiant energy. The parents wished the boy to be energetic in pursuing well being for himself, his family, his friends, and a successful career as well. Haipin would like her daughter to be a lovely, happy girl with the traditional Chinese merits of calmness and peace. These qualities would be popular in her search for relationships and a rewarding career as well. Haipin would like to name her baby girl Serene. Either a boy or a girl would have a mid-name in Chinese culture for keeping ethnic origin.

The spirits of the holiday season were filled with music on the radio stations, and with decorations in the streets at the retail stores. It was November and Haipin increased the frequency of visits to her obstetrician. The physician predicated either a Christmas or a New Year's baby for Haipin.

Haipin became uneasy, worrying about the safety of the baby that could be born at any time. The unfortunate happening of her two previous miscarriages was still lingering in her mind. She could not take the baby's safety and health for granted. Haipin tried to work hard to assure that she did not make any mistakes.

There was no way she could feel peace of mind unless her husband was around her most of the time and she was not alone at home. During the two weeks before the baby was due, Haipin wished that her husband could ask for leave without pay from his full-time employment, and at the same time get special permission to take the semester final examination when the students returned to college for spring term. In reality, she was aware that the chance to fulfill her wishes was not good. Still the baby might be born some time later than the prediction. Haipin found the only thing to release her anxiety was thinking positively, and let fate take care of the rest.

The cold weather with frost, ice, and snow is a normal, natural phenomenon in the Kansas prairie while entering November. People prepare for the joyous holiday season, celebrating Thanksgiving, then, Christmas, and New Year's Day. For the young couple, they would prepare to welcome a new member of their family.

The holiday season, plus the welcome of a newborn was indeed a double celebration for the young couple. Haipin, however, had sort of a lonesome feeling. She was homesick, missing her mother, brothers, sisters, and her fellow teachers, and good friends in Manila, as well as her new associates in Taiwan. Here in the college town no one was close enough as a friend/neighbor to plan a baby shower for her. The busy husband wished that a day could be composed of 28 hours so he could have the additional four hours totally devoted to Haipin and house chores. In reality, Haipin could not ask more from her poor husband. Anyone, such as Yan Yun, working full time with a muscle oriented job and at the same time taking a full time load of college work would be exhausted physically for doing anything else.

Haipin was glad that her husband had more time at home, since the college was in semester break. She needed that mostly for the preparation of taking care of their newborn baby. Though they could not afford to spend money on special food and house decoration for the coming Christmas, the couple was happy to see decoration on the streets and at the retail stores, the spirit of celebrating the big holiday. At the same time, Haipin had a feeling of something special, the joyous Christmas and the birth of her first child.

A few times, the couple was amid the crowd of Christmas shoppers. On a tight budget they could only buy limited decoration items for Christmas. Most of their spending had been on infant items. For Haipin, it was difficult for the once spoiled girl not to think of her beloved father while going shopping. Dad would pay for what she wished to buy. Now she must consider choosing an item with quality and low price. She wished she could have made more money before quitting the assembly line production job. She wished her dad was still alive, then she could have money to select the best item for her first baby.

Yan Yun had a couple of days off from Iowa Beef Processing for Christmas. The college was in semester break. Haipin was glad to have him around her for part of the holiday celebration. The couple spent Christmas Eve quietly at home. On Christmas Day, Katherine, a student form Hong Kong, who did not go out of town, visited with Haipin. Kathy was the only guest sharing holiday spirits with Haipin and her husband. Since Haipin was expecting a baby within a week, everyone wished Haipin good luck for a safe labor and delivery of a healthy baby.

In anticipating the New Year's Day baby, Yan Yun asked for a couple of days off from his employer so he could be available whenever Haipin needed help.

There was no symptom that Haipin would have a baby on New Year's Day (1971). She doubted the physician's prediction. Haipin thus let her husband go back to work. She did ask him to alert his supervisor for a possible emergency telephone call from home.

Though Haipin missed the chance to give birth on New Year's Day, she congratulated the mother whose newborn won the title; together with the headlines on the news media and gifts presented by the local business community. After New Year's Day, Haipin expected the moment of laboring at any time. She was happy to be a mother for the first time. Yet, she was nervous, worrying about the uncertainty of the delivery but wished for the best. On fulfilling a woman's motherhood responsibility, Haipin was ready to meet the challenge.

As the Family Grows ...

It was Monday, January 4th, 1971; a typical winter day; sunny, four degrees Fahrenheit in Emporia, Kansas. The college was still in semester break. Yan Yun, however, had to work his night shift at Iowa Beef. As he returned home from the car repair shop, Haipin was having labor pains. Yan Yun rushed her to the obstetrician's office. Then, as recommended by her physician, Yan Yun took her to the local Newman hospital.

Haipin checked in the hospital at five in the afternoon and was placed in a waiting room in the maternity department. Yan Yun was the only family member around. He was allowed to visit the room during the waiting. Here in the quiet small room, Haipin endured the labor pains, off and on. Looking at the wall there were pictures and diagrams of the baby's movement. A positive thinking about the new life she would bring to the family made Haipin feel better. Her husband's presence at the bedside warmed her heart.

Haipin lost the sense of time as the pains and contractions continued. However she could remember a short message to Yan Yan from the nurse,

"Sir, it is midnight. The baby moves slowly. We do not expect to be sending her to the delivery room soon. Go home, we will call you later."

Although Haipin's pain in the delivery room was intense, it was short. And the happiest moment was the doctor's announcement,

"It is a healthy baby boy."

The baby was born at 7:20 in the morning of January 5, 1971. It was more than 14 hours of labor after checking in at 5pm in the waiting room on January 4th to the birth of the newborn at 7:20 on January 5th. The baby Ray stood out alone with black hair with the rest of the babies (from Caucasian parents) in the newborn nursing room. A mid name Yuan-shin (the starting of a new year in Chinese) was immediately added to Ray's birth certificate.

Like a soldier wining a tough fighting battle, Haipin could not conceal her excitement on the triumphant reward, mother of a healthy baby boy.

Most new mothers return to work four weeks after giving birth to a baby. Haipin reported to a new job two weeks after leaving the hospital. She secured a job at Iowa Beef, the largest employer in town. Now the couple worked for the same employer on different shifts. Haipin started at seven o'clock in the morning, while

Yan Yun remained on the second shift, from 3:30 pm to midnight.

The increase of family expenses was a big pressure to the first time young mother, leaving her nursing care to a babysitter and hurried up to work outside the home. For Haipin, besides a career, she now faced a new challenge, and that was to take care of the baby.

Unless arrangement was made for a baby sitter, Haipin could not be free to do anything else. Unless the baby sitter was a good one, she would not have peace of mind. Lacking in childcare experience herself, and limited human resources for consultation, made Haipin sometimes frustrated in choosing a childcare person. She worried that her baby might be mistreated behind her back. Thus searching for a good baby sitter was to be Haipin's headache for years to come.

Haipin was in a hurry to find a baby sitter to take care of her two-week old infant child so that she could report to her new job, Haipin became frustrated in trying to find one. Some of the problems were the pay rate, distance from home, transportation, hours available, and baby food. She was almost close to making a decision to quit her newly secured job. In this moment, Haipin tried to call Betty Toso, her neighbor across the street. Though Betty would agree only to an emergency situation base, her rescue mission saved Haipin from losing a job. This was the first problem Haipin encountered since becoming a mother.

From now on, searching for a baby sitter or day care facility and visiting with the pediatrician clinic became regular. Though her husband would take the baby for a routine doctor's office visit most of the time, Haipin's hustle and bustle life had never changed, but increased more. In addition to working full time, cooking, laundry, typing college papers for her husband, she had another important responsibility, and that was taking care of the baby.

Haipin never had peace of mind for a long period of stability in securing a baby sitter. Some baby sitters were young mothers with their own infants. Others were retired grandmas with pets around the house. A daycare facility might have strict rules with many disadvantages against working parents. Once a young mother with a newborn son four days older than Ray, treated Ray differently from her own baby. She would not feed Ray as many times as he needed. The half full baby food jar that was left was evidence of the babysitter's unfair treatment. In a few cases, a baby food jar remained unopened. Haipin could not stand such unfair treatment for her child.

Once a retired single grandma accepted Haipin's offer for the babysitting job. It would be a good choice for any mother to see that a woman with valuable experience in raising kids was available for taking care of her child. The grandma lived in a comfortable house, which was another plus for the job. Haipin could not believe her eyes on how her child was treated by this seemingly kind and experienced child-nursing grandma. One day

Haipin went to the grandma's house, picking up her baby earlier than regular time. She heard a baby crying. As she peeped through the window, the three months old Ray was left on the living room floor near a large television set. The grandma might be in another room. Apparently the baby had a scare while he was sniffed over by a pet. As the grandma answered the door, the dog followed her. Haipin was very unhappy with the grandma's non-existent responsibility, but held her anger for a while. It took Hapin two weeks to find the grandma's replacement.

It is Haipin's belief and working ethics that poor performance on doing any job is not acceptable. Haipin always reported to a job on time and employed her best ability to maintain quality of work done. Since working as a production worker in American manufacturing plants, she received a good evaluation from UMCO Fishing Equipment Company. And here at Iowa Beef, she passed a probation period with high marks from her supervisor. Haipin continued working hard on her current job. She was among the top performance employees at Iowa Beef that rewarded a bonus check of $130 on her first Christmas with the new employer.

Haipin had no doubt sacrificed her romantic and peaceful family life with her husband. The young couple was always on the run. As a full time worker, a student spouse, a housewife, and a mother of an infant child, Haipin simply was hard pressed to find any spare time for enjoying things other than earning money or fulfilling obligations.

On a typical day, Haipin would sneak out of home for work at 6:30 in the early morning while her husband was still sound asleep. Another clock alarm sounded at about seven for Yan Yun. He must hurry for the college morning classes. At the same time he had to prepare the baby for the babysitter in a very short time. Before he got ready to work the second shift at Iowa Beef, he would be hurrying to take the baby home. This was the couple's happiest moment of the day. They had missed seeing Ray since leaving him at the babysitter's in the early morning.

Yan Yun usually returned home from work at midnight. Like a burglar he sneaked into the bedroom as quietly as possible, avoiding disturbing wife and child's sleep. However, baby crying could happen any time. Not enough sleep became ways of the couple's daily life.

Haipin attended her husband's graduation ceremony on earning his second Master's degree in August 1971. She wished that good luck would be with her husband as he started a professional career. Then she would no longer be a student wife, but a dedicated mother and secondary income partner of the family.

Unfortunately her expectation failed, her husband lost every effort to secure a job. Since Yan Yun's college preparation was for a higher education position, he sent more than a hundred applications to colleges and universities across the country, he got only a few responses by telephone inquiry. This was the most frustrating year. Haipin became less optimistic for the family's immediate financial release. She lowered her expectation for her husband securing a job, but enjoyed the substance of traveling with him. This is the best way to keep good spirits from a bad situation.

After a year long of disappointment in failing to find a new job, Yan Yun decided to go back to school for a teaching certification program that could lead him to hold a public school position. The certificate program was a 31-hour credit classroom and intern project. Thus he committed a full-time student load for another year. Haipin continued another year as a student wife and full-time employment as well.

Meanwhile, Haipin got pregnant again. For protecting her pregnancy she worked part time which would provide her some time for easing physical strain. The workaholic woman, however, would still like to have something to occupy her mind. As her pregnancy was still in an early stage, she thought she could take credit hours at the local college. Haipin enrolled as a part-time student, taking six hours in business. For the first time, the couple both attended the same college while working part time with the same employer, Iowa Beef.

In April 1973, after spring break, public school representatives began visiting the local college for preliminary job interviews. This time Haipin was optimistic about her husband's chance to find a teaching position in Kansas' schools, as he would be certified as a high school teacher just a few weeks away. As a result, several schools had invited him to visit school campuses to tour their facilities and meet faculty. This process serves as a final interview with the school principal, superintendent, or school board members. The prospect of employment is usually very good.

The couple visited many school campuses in Kansas on Yan Yun's job interviews. A job interview was the only out of town trip in the couple's hustle and bustle life. Since public schools would not pay travel expenses for the candidate, but considered it the applicant's responsibility, interviews were set on Saturdays. Haipin was glad that in some short distance travel, she would be able to go with her husband. They enjoyed these rare travel opportunities as a combined business and family recreation trip. All the family would travel in a car. Ray, their three year old son, would be excited, seeing the new picturesque country side scenery that he did not have a chance to see at a babysitter's in the city. It was also a quiet time for Haipin. Campus interviews, though expensive (mostly on gasoline), traveling with her husband could get rid of his loneliness and boredom from long hours of driving. Her husband's successful interview would be the family's ultimate goal.

Again, disappointments came one after another. Yan Yun's school campus interviews in Kansas City, the metropolitan area, as well as medium and small cities did not win a teaching contract. It was June 1973. Haipin worried about her husband's future. He completed the teaching certification program in May, but still no sight of securing a teaching position.

A long distance phone call reached the couple one evening, breaking the inactive status of job hunting. It was for Yan Yun. The Superintendent of Kansas Unified School District #234 (Kirwin-Agra) invited Yan Yun to visit the school campus for a job interview. Yan Yun was impressed by the Superintendent's interest in him while conducting the first interview on the college campus in early May.

Haipin was excited over the news. It might be husband's delayed school appointment. She would not mind settling down in a rural community. Kirwin - Agra are both small farm towns in the open space of the western Kansas prairie. Agra, where the high school is located had a population of 300 at that time. The district office at Kirwin was not much bigger. For an immigrant, finding the first professional job is tough. Thus Haipin did not have much expectation of her husband returning home with a teaching contract.

Haipin did not go with her husband for this interview as she usually did at previous interviews. Her pregnancy at this stage had made her a little uncomfortable being buckled in a seat in a small car for a 400 plus miles round trip travel. She stayed at home with her three-year-old son for a quiet, yet sort of anxious day. She prayed for her husband's best performance while meeting with members of the school board.

"Papa!" Ray alerted Haipin's attention that Daddy might be at the door while the doorbell was ringing.

Yes, it was. Yan Yun hugged his wife and son, happily announcing, "I got the job" waving his hands with the teaching contract with the signatures of the school board president and the superintendent as well.

Haipin finally had a sense of security for the future. She was glad to see her husband starting a new career. His six years of student life in the United States was long enough; it was time for a change. Haipin could now, if not permanently, resign the student wife position. During the last five years she worked full time supporting her husband and family. As her second child was on the way, Haipin needed more time at home.

Although her husband's low starting salary at a rural school would not be able to provide a better living for the family, it did make a whole lot of change on his credit to get loans. The couple needed a good performing car for moving the family to the new location. Living in the open space country, a less troubled car probably would make Haipin and her family feel safer while driving on the remote country roads. Thus the couple decided to buy a new car.

Haipin could not believe that her husband's teaching contract had such secure power. Knowing that Yan Yun had earned a Master's degree from the local college and had accepted a new teaching job, a car dealership in the college town persuaded the couple to purchase a current year (1973) Oldsmobile Omega. And without any question, a local bank approved the loan of $3,300. Yan Yun's annual salary for the new position was under $7,000. This new model car was considered very expensive for the first year teacher. For a while, Haipin was not comfortable spending loan money on such a luxury item. As time went by, America's debt living style became more acceptable to her.

It was quite a change of feeling in moving the family since the last relocation from Norman, Oklahoma to Emporia, Kansas. This time the couple moved out from the city to a small rural farm town. Now Haipin was a mother of a three-year-old child and was three-month's pregnant. Since the family could not afford to rent a furnished apartment, they must have some furniture for their new residence. They found bargain prices on used furniture at a flea market and pawnshops. Somebody's trash became Haiping's treasure. For the first time the couple had their own mattress, dinner table, chairs, crib, etc. Therefore they would not be able to move the family in a small sedan any more.

Haipin and her husband began to learn how to move a family for less. Basically there are two options. The simple one is to rent a truck with the size that would fit your cargo needs. You do everything; packing, loading, unloading, driving, and you may be on the road all the time. The other is to let the moving company handle the entire operation. This option costs more, and you have to follow their schedule, someone must be available to receive the cargo at the new residence, or you have to go to a storage facility to claim your cargo. The advantage is that you feel a peace of mind.

Neither Haipin nor her husband would be able to drive a standard manual truck. The family had limited resources to pay for moving. There was only a few options left for them. After consultation with a moving company, the couple agreed to a flexible schedule of delivery within a period of two months. The moving company would load the couple's cargo whenever they had room in a run that was heading in that direction. Yan Yun had notified the landlord of his new residence to receive his cargo, and at the same time notified the trucking company.

Yes, for many years since coming to the United States, Haipin, for the first time had a sense of less uncertainty about the family's future. The couple had been granted U.S. permanent resident status. Her husband had just started his first professional position with a potential of prosperity in the teaching career. She could have peace of mind in raising their kids.

In July 1973, about three weeks before school classes began, Yan Yun moved his family to the small remote farm town of Agra, where he would teach at the local high school. Haipin then would be a full time housewife, taking a break from years of hard work at the assembly line in a manufacturing facility.

Haipin looked at the cute, small community of Agra with a fresh view and compared it to the cities. It also reminded her of the small mountain mining town where she held her first teaching position in the local public school in Taipei County, Taiwan. The population of 300 in Agra was not that small in comparison to elsewhere. Here she could breathe fresh air, not polluted as in the mining town, or in the cities.˙ Residents of Agra could reach outside communities through good highways and county roads as well.

Haipin and her family's residence in the small town, Agra, became a big local news around the town. Never before had there been a non-Caucasian family in this early German settlement. As the school district welcomed the new teacher, Yan Yun, from China, the neighbors were ready to meet his family. Some would drop by and have a little chat with Haipin, others waved their hands at her while Haipin was taking a walk with her son in the quiet streets.

To live in a rural small village was a new experience for Haipin. She did not have a house number and street name, but the smart postal worker could send a special deliver mail to her. Walking to the local U.S. Post Office to pick up mail became a part of her daily life. The church, the bank, the only grocery store, the city hall (in one small house), and the gasoline station, were all within a short walking distance. The city hall had only one full time employee. He might be called a service master. His job covered duties that police, fireman, custody of waste dumping site, ... would do. Residents of the small village probably did not have a full time mayor. Haipin once dropped in the city hall and found the mayor was a part time housewife. Curiously Haipin was surprised to find out that the city hall had a bookshelf with a set of encyclopedia, an unabridged Webster's dictionary, and small number of children's books.

Most residents in this rural community spent their leisure time in outdoor recreation. The popular ones were hunting, boating, and fishing. Yan Yun never owned firearms, neither was he interested in hunting sports. Nearby Agra, there was a big lake known as Kirwin Lake, the National Wildlife Reservation. It was a major outdoor recreation center for residents of surrounding communities. Occasionally on the weekends, Haipin and her husband would take son Ray to the lake, strolling along the lakeshore. The fishing scene reminded Haipin of her first job in the United States as a fishing equipment employee at UMCO, in Cape Girardeau, Missouri. Once Yan Yun tried to spend his spare time fishing. Haipin supported his idea. Unfortunately he never did go a second time, after the first failed trial, four-hours of fishing without getting anything.

The sudden change of living environment from crowded streets, heavy traffic highways, and hustle and bustle of city life, to a small quiet peaceful village in the open space prairie, had given Haipin a chance to think about her priorities and family, and career for the future. Her pregnancy had kept her from participating in some activities. It was actually a much needed break for taking care of her family and, above all, the coming of a new baby. Anyway she began to like the rural living.

The hospitality and friendly neighbors of the small community moved Haipin. Knowing she was expecting a Christmas baby, the high school principal's wife, as well as the school superintendent sponsored a baby shower for Haipin. More than forty neighbors came to greet the new mother-to-be just three weeks before Christmas Day 1973. She got presents from neighbors, receiving almost everything she needed for the newborn. In contrast, Haipin did not have a shower celebration at the city of Emporia for her first baby. She did receive a gift from Mrs. M. Sullivan, a faculty member of the college. Yan Yun once took a class with her.

Residents in this region were not surprised to have subzero temperatures during the Christmas season. However this winter (1973), consecutive subzero weather had been lingering for a month. Snow was everywhere. Haipin was ready to welcome the new baby. At this time, she expected the laboring hour could be any moment. She was concerned about the snowstorm and icy streets and highways that could make the ten-mile drive to the local hospital difficult for her husband. In the rural area emergency help was not as easy to get as in the city in general, and at night in particular.

The expected 'Christmas Day baby' was yet five days away. In the early morning on December 20, Haipin had labor pains. Not until 10 o'clock was she sure the time was right for going to the hospital. Her first child-laboring experience helped her on this matter.

Meanwhile Yan Yun got a temporary substitute for his class and rushed Haipin to the hospital. It was a cloudy day without accumulation of snow. He completed check-in registration with the hospital and resumed a class lecture at school. Less than an hour upon returning to the classroom, Yan Yun got a call from the principal's office,

'Congratulations! Mr. Li, your wife has a baby girl,' Mrs. Wallace, the school secretary, told the happy father.

Haipin was glad to find out that this labor lasted less than one hour, as compared to her first child's labor of 14 hours. The baby girl was healthy and many said she looked like her Daddy. Haipin named their daughter, Joy, instead of the earlier selected name of Serene. Joy's mid name was Shirling (bell ringing on the snow-covered open field.)

Haipin returned home from the hospital two days before Christmas. Outside was still subzero temperature, with a foot high of snow that stayed unchanged since the first big snowstorm a couple of weeks ago. Inside the home, the new parents were warm in hearts, a happy family, welcoming a new member, Joy. The three-year old brother, though curious about the new baby, kissed his sister whenever she was crying. Although the couple did not have relatives around and friends nearby, they prepared a tea party, inviting next door neighbors and one couple from out of town on Christmas Eve. They wished to share happiness with guests on such a joyous holiday.

The spring finally came to this small town. Once snow covered open fields turned to green trees and lawns. Yan Yun decided to find a teaching position elsewhere in Kansas public schools. He had in mind professional advancement as well as social life. Haipin thus was ready for another move.

In the spring semester, 1974, Haipin, and her two little kids would accompany her husband on most job interview trips. His job-hunting business travel gave Haipin a much-needed break from routine household chores in the quiet small village.

On the 24th of May, 1974 Yan Yun successfully landed a new position at Atchison (Kansas) High School. It meant for Haipin another time of relocation. In the couple's frequent mobility so far, it was a short stay as a new resident in the small village of Agra.

With the family growing bigger to four members and the increase of household belongings, the couple faced a big moving expense for a mover with limited available funds. Most businesses, including moving and storage companies did not have local offices. It was hard to get a bargain while discussing pricing with the customer who was not a native English speaker by telephone communication.

The topic of moving became a hot debate between husband and wife. Haipin insisted on taking all kitchen stuff and children's toys, plus furniture bought from the junkyard to their new residence in the city, while Yan Yun wished to get rid of them in order to save moving expenses. It was a matter of convenience, versus saving money. Fortunately, they were lucky to settle the debate without losing their points.

The help came from the local community. Knowing that Haipin would move to a new residence in northeastern Kansas area, Dixon, a neighbor village resident, agreed to do the move with his own truck. He would charge $100, plus gasoline for this 500-mile round trip. Haipin and her husband were excited over this kind 'neighbor helps neighbor' assistance that might be found only in small towns. Instead of meeting the moving company's schedule, Dixon's assistance was very special. Dixon would help the couple load and unload all cargo. He planned to get to the destination the same day as Haipin and her family. There was no contract paper to sign. It was simply an old-fashioned honest business deal. Haipin was glad that she had the household stuff when the family moved in their new apartment. Dixon's truck traveled along with the family all the way.

'From six states and China' was the headline of a news article in the local newspaper the day Yan Yun started the new school year at Atchison (Kansas) Public Schools. Haipin was curious about her husband's name being featured in this story. Though Atchison with a population of 22,000 at that time, they had someone from China working at their local schools. Later Haipin sensed a community spirit in her new residence. She was invited to a school sponsored faculty/staff picnic at Jackson Park, and later a picture of her little kids appeared in the community paper.

Haipin enjoyed being a full-time housewife, taking care of kids and free from typing Yan Yun's college paper. However, her husband's school paycheck was simply too little to meet the growing family expenses. Instead of constantly waiting for Yan Yun's next month's paycheck, Haipin decided to go back to full-time employment for additional income. It was a difficult decision to make. She would not like to see her two young kids, the three-year old son and the newborn baby daughter under the care of someone she knew little about. However the hardship of family finance was distressful. Although Haipin's choice was reluctant, she did not have a better alternative.

Babysitting her next-door neighbor's two kids at Haipin's apartment was in her mind first. She would take care of her own kids and at the same time earn a few dollars and cents from caring for her neighbor's kids.

Haipin accepted Linda, her next door neighbor's offer for taking care of her two kids; Robert, 12, and Daniel, 4. The total package of payment, including food was $12 per week. Haipin was excited over the offer knowing she could earn easy money at home.

On the contrast, Haipin later found it was a big disappointment. The $12 could barely cover the cost of food. She could get very little help for her financial difficulty from babysitting. What Haipin got was a headache in trying to control the undesirable activity of the 12-year old. Robert would like to play outdoors with neighbor kids his age most of the time. Haipin, with eyes on the other three kids in the house, was not able to monitor Robert's outdoor activity. She worried that her responsibility of the boy's safety might be in jeopardy.

The once considered easy money earned by babysitting was no longer an alternative for the mother of two small kids. Haipin decided to go back to a manufacturing production job. She did very well at previous employment. The income was better and she would be free from the constant strain of the child safety responsibility of being a childcare worker.

Diagnosis With No Merits

As she focused on finding additional income to help the family financial hardship, Haipin was dismayed by the sudden illness of her son. The three-old lovely boy, Ray, had not had smiles for several days, and he cried most of the day. The lack of nursing experience and available consultations from relatives or knowledgeable friends made Haipin miserable in searching for a better solution before visiting a physician. Every mother knows that infant care is a consistent daily work, and baby crying is a routine. Haipin did not believe her son had a serious problem, but a minor discomfort due to a cold. However, she couldn't afford to risk the possibility of it becoming a problem. Anyway, she took the boy to see a family physician for a diagnosis. After examining the child, the doctor immediately recommended a surgical procedure at the hospital to remove a possible inflamed appendix. The physician said he found that the child had a 75% possibility of an appendix inflammation. Haipin and her husband could not find a second opinion on this matter, and thus put their signatures on the operation agreement.

The surgical procedure was undergone at 11 o'clock in the morning of September 20, 1974 at the local Atchison Hospital. The operation was successful, as claimed by the physician. Appendix had been removed. Surprisingly the surgeon admitted that he made a mistaken diagnosis. Haipin and her husband felt betrayed by the surgeon for his unethical mal practice that made heir son suffer at such a young age. The physician, however, defended his decision saying that the surgery would not harm the child's health, and the child could avoid the procedure later in his life.

Ray was dismissed from the hospital in six days. He was asked to come back to the physician's office for a post surgery evaluation. He should be completely recovered. However, this routine checkup turned out not as good as expected. Ray had to be back again to the clinic for another minor treatment. Knowing that the parents were not happy about his work, the physician did not express any kind of apologetic tone, but blaming the parents' lack of medical wisdom. Haipin believed that sort of racial discrimination with immigrants from another culture might be in the doctor's mind.

Helmet, Steel Top Shoes, And Heat

After Ray's total recovery from surgery, Haipin began to search for employment. She was lucky to know that The Rockwell International Metal Casting Division, a large manufacturing facility was located in a short walking distance from her apartment residence. Although she doubted her chances to get hired by the male dominated work force heavy equipment factory, she never forgot 'seeing is believing' motto. The good pay with the short walk-to-work distance was a strong force behind her pursuance.

As Haipin walked in the employment office, the clerk at the information desk was curious about the cute slim woman coming to apply for a predominately male, muscle based machinery worker and smiled at her,

"Hi, Ms. may I help you? We don't have
vacancies other than production workers
at the Foundry Department."

"Sir, I really don't have a particular job in mind.
I would like to work on any position available
for which I might be qualified. I wish to learn
new skills."

Haipin had no idea how much physical strength a worker in the foundry department required. But she did not wish to lose the chance to secure a job there. She convinced the office clerk that she could improve her strength at the job at a slow pace. Finally she was allowed to fill out an application. An interview schedule with the foreman had been set before she left the employment office.

The job interview came. Haipin was very nervous. She never had such an uneasy feeling in previous job interviews. Apparently, here a worker's strength was a basic requirement for handling heavy machinery. How could she defend her rather weak (female) status and less muscular appearance before the muscular foreman? Even if she got hired, how long could she survive at the job?

However, Haipin would not let the opportunity go away. She realized that pessimistic feelings would not help anything, but only ruin her attempt to get a new job. She wished to turn the less qualified status into a successful adventure.

Haipin walked into the conference room in the employment office. In contrast to her presumption of a strong, muscular tall guy, the foreman was a medium size gentleman in a blue worker's uniform. It was a surprise for the foreman to see, for the first time, a small slim female walking into the room for a job interview. It was even harder for him to believe that a woman would like to work in the foundry department.

"Haipin, you must be a person with confidence and determination. We currently don't have any female worker's among our workforce in the foundry shop. "

The foreman smiled at her, doubting her physical strength to do the job.

"Honestly speaking, I cannot say how good or how bad I could do something that is new to me. I'm sure you have a probation period for new workers. This would help you t o evaluate the performance of a new worker. If I have a chance to start my probation, I would do my best not to disappoint you. The success of my previous experience at UMCO was evidence of my commitment to the best of my ability."

Haipin rationalized her potential of doing a good job here if hired, and her quest for the foreman's understanding seemed to be working. After a short chat, the foreman took Haipin for a walk-through tour of the foundry's production floor.

She was given a steel helmet, a pair of safety boots, protective eyeglasses, and shock protection ear unit. It was a huge building equipped with rails at the ceiling and various sized machine lathes on the floor. The foreman stopped at a workstation where a crane was lifting and moving steel parts from one station to another. Haipin had no idea how long it would take her to become a good productive worker if hired. She could image how hard it would be to live with a helmet, the uncomfortable shoes, the heavy uniform, gloves, and tools every work day. The most uncomfortable encounter was the heat from the big steel melding unit. The big fans would not help much for relieving the burning heat. During the short walk through tour Haipin had conflicting views about this job. She needed income to help solve the family financial hardship, yet, the job was not a good one for a woman who was not strong. One of the worst things that could happen was a work-related accident. While in the process of handling heavy steel, a tired worker is vulnerable to an accident. In fact, she could not see any other female workers on the entire floor. What was her chance to be hired, only God knows. Anyway she decided to be positive on the matter for better or for worse should she get the job.

After the short tour, the foreman asked for Haipin's personal views on this kind of job.

"Sir, it is certainly a very challenging job. I have never had experience in working at a steel works, but I would like to meet the challenge if offered," Haipin answered positively without hesitation.

"Congratulations! Haipin, you are a courageous woman. I welcome you to join my staff You will fill a vacancy of a crane operator delivering steel to lathes on the main floor."

The foreman then handed Haipin a note for the personnel office and asked her to complete hiring procedures with the benefits coordinator. She was scheduled to be back for a two-day orientation. Then, a three-month probation would follow.

Working full time for a major corporation with comparatively good pay (starting hourly wage $3.35) and fringe benefits was a hard-to-believe event for the poor immigrant family. Haipin and her husband temporarily put away the risk of the workplace and got ready for her new job.

The mother of two young children had only one week to arrange for a babysitter for her kids before she could work. Haipin and her husband had just moved to the new city a couple of months ago. They lacked the social contact resources to find a good babysitter with the cost they could afford. Haipin never imaged how difficult it would be to work on this matter. As the time drew closer to her orientation schedule Haipin was in a very anxious state of mind. She was afraid of losing the opportunity that could improve the family financial situation, though mother's love of her kids was always her priority. The dilemma went on until Sunday, October 6, 1974 before she reported to work on the next Monday. The retired grandmother next door offered an emergency help with babysitting. She agreed to take care of Haipin's two kids for a short time, providing Haipin would not slow down her search for a nanny.

Haipin was glad that the two-day orientation was over. Nothing could be reported as exciting on the new job except for a very tired body. The uniform unit (the steel helmet, safety shoes, protective eye ware) alone was heavy enough to exhaust her energy. Standing at the workstation all the time was another source of feeling uncomfortable. At this moment if she could find something to release her negative feeling, it was the fact they could pay the bills. Anyway the steel works job came to her by choice. She was young and capable of surviving. She was willing to take the challenge.

Haipin could not believe she was a heavy machine (crane) operator whose job was to deliver steel. The first two days on the job, though they did not count as regular production, she began to taste how much pain she would be bearing physically. Haipin returned home with toes hurting from the heavy steel shoes and sore arms.

However, after she was on the job for a while she had a different view on what she was doing. Haipin spent most of her time pushing buttons, and moving handles on the control board. She had confidence in what she did. Even if she was not better than her male colleagues, she could do as good as the average good workers. It was nothing to do with muscle strength, but the mind. In this case, whenever there was not much choice for her, Haipin thought only of the opportunity.

The improvement of family income could be seen with their bank account in just a few weeks as Haipin worked through the probation period. Instead of worrying about insufficient funds most of the time, their joint checking account began to have a safe level of balance in the black. A part of Hairpin's weekly payroll check would go to a new savings account. A feeling of reward on hard work came from her happy family reunion at home with her kids and husband in the evenings and weekends after Haipin's long absence during the day.

Sometimes she did miss her childhood as a spoiled girl and later enjoyed the respectable position as a teacher in the Chinese schools in Manila. Haipin, however, never regretted her choice of marriage to a soldier/student and the career changes to a blue-collar worker. She believed that 'a job is a job.' There is difficulty in defining one better than another. Haipin only considers the opportunity at the time, and would overcome things that might need improvement.

None of her blue-collar colleagues at the foundry shop would look for long time teamwork with Haipin. They did not believe she could survive the heat and dust working environment any longer than the three months probation. On other consideration, they did like to keep a female worker at the male dominant- world. They would like to make jokes with her. Haipin welcomed the male crew's attention. With her positive attitude toward the job and nice personality she was very popular. She was a workaholic too. Haipin would like to accept overtime work assignments that some co-workers might turn down. She not only survived the harsh probation period, but also received the foreman's good remarks on hiring evaluation. Her employment had changed the supervisor's skeptical view on the female fitness in a male dominant workplace.

The Unthinkable Seconds

It was just about time to celebrate Haipin's first anniversary on the job with Rockwell International; she was proud of her success. She got along well with co-workers, had a good job performance, and, most significantly, had a safety record that she thought could never be done well at the heavy steel equipment manufacturer. Minor injuries on the job are not rare. She heard of one fatal accident recently.

On her routine crane operator job, in the afternoon just back form lunch break, all of a sudden Haipin felt unusually less sensitive on one of her legs from knee cap to the ankle. When she rolled up a little of her uniform pants, she found a purple spot about four inches in length on her leg. The line leader reported immediately to the foreman and she was escorted to the medical first aid unit. She was diagnosed as receiving a wound by a steel bar that slipped on her leg. The nurse on the scene had a first evaluation of her injury, it did not show evidence of broken bones. After emergency first aid treatment Haipin was sent home for a two-day paid leave. She was advised to go to the hospital should anything happen beyond her current condition.

Haipin did see a specialist regarding her work injury and was treated at the clinic with several visits. She was glad to find out that her employer paid medical bills and her wages. Though she suffered injury, she did not loose her income that was so essential for her family to survive. Compared to her husband's health benefits with limited coverage, her corporation's was a lot better than that of the public schools. She began to think the blue-collar job had its merits, thus would not think too much of her previous career as a teacher before coming to the United States.

It was unfortunate that Haipin had the accident, it also could have been a much worse injury in just a matter of unthinkable seconds. However the courageous workaholic woman viewed her life in a different way. She looks at life as a continuous struggle for better, not worse. Haipin never thought to slow down her work at Rockwell International due to the injury. Upon receiving the physician's report of her full recovery, Haipin returned to a 40-hour regular load and won her supervisor's overtime assignment as well. Productivity that meets quality and quantity requirements is always a manufacturing industry's goal. Being a good worker, Haipin was frequently given overtime work as a monetary reward.

Through Haipin's hard work at Rockwell, her family savings in the bank grew at a slow but steady pace. In the summer of 1975, about six months since Haipin's new employment, the couple would be able to make a down payment of $3,000 on owning a $10,000 old house. Both Haipin and her husband's full time employment would qualify them for getting a mortgage loan from local banks. To own a house had been the immigrant couple's dream. However they did not think that their dream could come true this early in their career.

Surprisingly Haipin's decision to buy a house came from her next door neighbor, the lovely Mrs. Louise Pecker. They had been friends since Haipin and her family moved in the 500 block of Park Street. The retired widow lived with her granddaughter, Tammy, a second grader in school. The grandma would like to baby sit Haipin's kids on emergency occasions.

Louise, 78, recently was not in good health. One of her wishes was to sell her long time home to a friend. Haipin was her choice. Haipin could save commission cost because no other salesman was involved. Though the half-century-old construction needed a lot of repair work, Haipin considered the good price ($10,000), a savings, since there would be no distance moving, and her ability to pay was an offer she did not wish to pass away.

'Wow! My Home'

On August 2, 1975, Haipin and her family moved to their newly bought old house. For so many years the couple moved from one apartment to another. They never had a feeling of home.

Probably owning a house is one of the most common dreams for an immigrant. And the young couple's became true earlier than they expected. Haipin was proud of her contribution to this property ownership. Her current full time employment with Rockwell International helped to build savings that made the purchase possible. As Mrs. Louise Pecker handed the house key to Haipin, she had a sense of having a shelter to be called 'home'. Though some apartments where she once lived had better physical condition than this old house, Haipin never had a feeling of 'home', until today.

Moving had never been as easy as relocating next door, from house 513 to 515 on the same side of Park Street. Haipin and her husband never thought about being tired after weeks of working, but put everything in place and decorated the house. Instead they were in high spirits thinking of more house improvement projects. In two years they added a room air conditioner and repaired the single-car garage. The sense of a 'sweet home' touched Hapin's heart while walking home from work, physically tired from daylong work, but happy to hug her kids and husband at their newly owned home.

Haipin continued to seek overtime work, either voluntarily or mandatory that made her one of a few high paid workers on the production team. It also made her savings account at the bank grow steadily.

To an immigrant family that lacks human resources to support, the foundation of happiness might come from financial stability. Haipin built on that foundation. She could not make this happen if she declined to accept blue-collar employment. She would not make more income if she were not willing to accept overtime assignments.

The stability of family income leads to a happy family life. Haipin now could afford to pay a babysitter for caring for her two kids so she could work full time. The family would be able to pay monthly utility bills without waiting for husband's payday. Yan Yun thus could go back to school as a part-time student working on his doctorate degree at the University of Kansas. Now Haipin carried out the responsibility as wife, mother, blue-collar worker and a minor role as a student's wife again.

Everyone knows that working on a job is the best way to hold the position more secure. However it is also true that no job is immune from dismissal by an employer if the business environment changes. Haipin kept her positive attitudes toward her employment, but would always prepare for the worst if unluckily she might be laid off. She had been reassigned different job positions in different departments. At times she asked to work part-time, or switched from day to night schedule. Haipin was lucky that she survived a big reduction of workforce in 1976. She worked there only one year and did not have any advantage in seniority.

After survival of the big layoff, Haipin was back to her mind of normalcy. The next exciting thing was to prepare for her son's first year of school at a nearby kindergarten. The hard working mother was fortunate to get help from a very nice babysitter, Mrs. Joy Goodman. Joy agreed to take care of Haipin's two kids, Ray and Joy at her home during hours that the couple was at work. She also would take Ray to and from school in the afternoon.

In early open house days, Haipin and her husband visited Washington Elementary School about half a mile from home. They met the kindergarten teacher who would teach the first year new student class. Ray, though a little shy, showed no sign of withdrawing while answering the teacher's greeting and while chatting with other kids.

It was a special day for Haipin. She was eager to go home and hug her son. Ray's first kindergarten class was held in the afternoon, Tuesday, August 17, 1977. As Haipin got home, the kids and her husband stood at the front door greeting the hardworking mom.

"Mammy, I did not cry. My teacher said I am a good boy. " Ray told his mom about activities at school.

Then the three-year old Joy asked her mother: "Can I go to school with my brother?"

The innocent kids' talk warmed mother's heart. Haipin promised to spend some time at the park with them and eat at McDonalds the coming weekend. She did not sign overtime work on that day.

There was another day special to the family. Haipin never forgot the big event in her life on that day. On October 12, 1977, she and her husband took oath to become naturalized American citizens at U. S. District Court of Kansas. It was indeed a long period of waiting to be an American. Yan Yun had been in the U. S. A. as an alien for ten years. Haipin, holding a student spouse visa, entered the port of entrance in Honolulu a year later in 1968. If you are an alien, you never have the feeling of being at home, though you own a house.

There was a big crowd witnessing the ceremony. More than 60 petitions from 25 countries of the world raised their hands while repeating the oath led by the judge. Another unforgettable scene was the large number of cheering friends and relatives that came to offer their best wishes for the new citizens.

Every new citizen received a certificate, a welcome letter with President Jimmy Carter's signature on it, a small American flag, and an information handbook about rights and obligations a new citizen should know. All new citizens were busy in taking pictures around the federal court building for remembering this important historical moment in their life.

The Triumph of Sharing

It seemed that life for the young hard working couple was getting better as time went by. After a series of exciting events of becoming an American citizen, another special day came to this immigrant family. Yan Yun would be earning a doctorate degree at the University of Kansas. Haipin, a long time student wife, had been a strong supporter of his education from undergraduate to a university terminal degree program. She was proud of her husband's success in academic attainment and thus was egotistical of her contributions to make it possible.

Haipin with son 7, and daughter, 4, was invited as a candidate's family guest by University of Kansas 1978 commencement program to attend the graduation ceremony. She considered the program special because it was a separate doctoral hooding ceremony held in a small theater on the university campus by the School of Education, and that her husband was the candidate to receive a diploma.

It was not the first time that Haipin attended her husband's graduating ceremony. She was among the crowded audience to applaud graduates holding certificates while walking down from the podium at Yan Yun's B.A., M. A., M.L.S. college degrees. However this one was special. There was live violin music while the candidate received the diploma. Though Haipin was excitied to see her husband and other candidates awarded with academic degrees, she was nervous and held her breath until the ceremony was over. She found no other kids younger than her daughter in the audience. She was relieved that her daughter did not cry or made any noise that might interrupt the tranquility of the ceremony.

Immediately after the doctoral hooding ceremony, the couple and kids rushed to the university grand commencement with over 4,000 graduates at the football field. Drizzle did not shorten the ceremony, and everyone got wet. Haipin would never forget this day, May 22, 1978 when her husband reached his highest academic attainment, the earning of a doctoral degree. She was proud to share her husband's triumph of accomplishments, and that her contributions had helped in reaching this goal. She would be no longer a student wife, but with full energy devoted to being a good wife, a good mother, and a career woman.

EIGHT

The Unsettled Years

Chapter Eight

The energetic husband had no intention of settling down with his family after earning a doctorate degree. He sent many applications for a university position, but seldom received returned mail in his favor. Rejections never bothered him.

Haipin however had reasons to stay in Atchison for a while. The couple had just bought a used house, kids began school, and Haipin had a good job. Though it was her intent not to relocate soon, it would be hard for her to reject her husband's pursuance for career advancement.

On August 16, 1978, the new school year just began. Yan Yun came home not telling her about new things taking place in his high school; about his consideration to resign from his current job. Haipin was shocked at first, thinking he might be fired. Later it turned out to be exciting news regarding his search for a college position.

Yan Yun got a call from Southwestern Oklahoma State University concerning his last interview for the assistant professor position. The university would offer the job provided he would accept the offer and assume the teaching assignment in two weeks. It was sort of an emergency appointment. Yan Yun considered the offer as a good opportunity, one not to be overlooked. He confirmed his acceptance immediately on the phone.

The first class of the new semester was on Monday, August 29th. Yan Yun must leave for the new job in a week. It did not give Haipin much time to think about the new change. Meanwhile she was aware that it could take months to move the family down to Oklahoma. She anticipated problems that would be facing her. The family had only one car and it served her husband's transportation needs for his new job and his weekend home visits. Haipin began to wonder how those single moms lived their life. Now she faced a similar situation, her husband would live in a city more than 400 miles away from home. She was the only adult at home for a while.

The Hustle Besieged Mom

It was not an easy job for Haipin to take care of two kids and at the same time work full time outside the home. The family had only one car that her husband took to Oklahoma. There were no close friends she could ask for help in time of need.

On a normal weekday, Haipin began to fight the hustle and bustle war when the alarm clock went off in the morning. She had less than one hour to dress the kids, and to get baby food ready for the baby sitter to pick up. During the cold days, pulling the kids from a warm bed was a fight resulting in their crying and resisting cooperation.

It could be a bad day when the babysitter had car trouble, overslept, or just not in a good mood, thus showing up late. Haipin, being an on time, punctual production worker, would not only feel guilty for reporting late to her station and getting a warning note from her supervisor, but also the loss of pride of having perfect attendance. The guilt of forcing the kids to get up early was hurting the loving mom.

Nor, at the end of the day of working on the production line would she get much of a break at home. She would engage in busy work taking care of kids: cooking dinner, doing laundry, preparing kids' lunch, helping kids with showers. In fact, she could not relax until the kids went to bed.

But nothing was hurting the mother's feelings more than when the foreman told Haipin of the babysitter's call that her kids did not feel well. Perhaps it is the nature of young kids that their immune systems are not strong. Haipin had a few such calls at work. To keep her feeling better Haipin started her daily work with a silent prayer, wishing her kids well and that soon the family could all be together.

Kids always eagerly kept their fingers crossed for the weekend, hoping Daddy would take them to the park and eat at McDonalds. They could not understand why he could not come home every weekend. Haipin had stopped signing up for overtime work since Yan Yun took the new job in Oklahoma. However, her mobility was very limited without a car. Haipin was uncomfortable listening to the kids' complaints.

"Mommy, can we play at the park? "
"Mommy, why not buy a car?"
"Could we take a walk to McDonalds?"
"Could you buy me new toy? I am a good kid."

Haipin could not help thinking how hard life was for those single moms everyday. Compared to them, her experience was rather short, about three months. Yan Yun made final arrangements to move the family south to Oklahoma, the state with booming oil and gas drilling at that time, the late 1970s. The target date would be during the Thanksgiving holiday weekend. More good news to the hard working mother was the purchase of a new brick house by her professor husband in the university town where the couple would reside.

Haipin never had a chance to choose the place where she wished to live, nor could her husband. It was her husband's career development that dictated relocations. At this point, she was happy that the 'single mom' type life would be ended soon. Yet she was not sure she could ever find a job that required her education background. Haipin was not an American educated person, but a foreign made product. She doubted she could use her previous blue-collar labor experience to find a job in a beef processing firm, a fishing equipment company, or heavy steel products manufacturing industry. However she was willing to learn a new trade in the new community.

The family belongings grew bigger each time they moved from one place to another. They tried a new approach in moving this time. Instead of paying the mover Company, they rented a medium size truck. It would save the cost and time waiting for the furniture to arrive. The couple asked a real estate company to put their Atchison home on the market for sale and got ready for the new, exciting, yet worrisome adventure of moving to Oklahoma.

The couple made this moving plan. Yan Yun would drive the Ryder rental truck with all heavy articles loaded. Haipin shared moving duty by driving their family sedan, a 1973 Omega. In order to keep the kids busy during the long drive, Ray, 7, would sit beside Dad, and daughter, Joy, 4, with Mom. Kids also had an assignment. The brother and sister would relay parents' messages through walkie-talkies.

It was the time of year, latter part of November, that bad weather, snow or ice, could happen in this area any time. The couple's wishes for a nice day on the moving trip did not come true. They left their Atchison home on Saturday, November 25th, 1978 south-bound on I-35. The rain was off and on all day. Haipin was nervous because she had never driven so far.

There was no car trouble or traffic slow down during morning hours until the couple reached Emporia. As they tried to resume the trip south after taking a short break at a roadside gas station, Yan Yun could not start the truck. The weatherman gave no prediction of any change for a clear sky that day or the next. Since the mechanic was not on duty that day, the couple wished for a miracle that they could get help from someone.

Yes, by surprise a traveler driving a truck stopped and kindly extended a helping hand. He said he was not an auto mechanic, but would like to make a trial. He then took several tools from his truck and worked on the couple's rental truck. The seemingly dead engine started running again. Haipin and her husband continued their travel south along Interstate 35.

Another bad situation happened when the family car fleet passed Wichita, the major city in southern Kansas. It was dark, at heavy traffic hour on a rainy day and on slippery roads. The bad visibility prevented Haipin from following the truck that her husband tried to keep a short distance from her. Meanwhile the walkie-talkies did not work and the kids were tired and fell asleep. Haipin got lost when she took the wrong exit. The most unthinkable thing in the couple's minds was an auto accident in unknown streets of a metropolitan city.

Yan Yun signaled to exit to a roadside service station when he passed Wichita's traffic jammed city streets. He did not have any idea whose car was following, but was nervous, with his heart pounding, praying for Haipin's safety in case she was not in that car.

As he pulled his rental truck through the lighted island, Yan Yun identified the car that followed his was an Omega and the woman that walked out from the vehicle was Haipin.

"Thank God! We made it!"

The couple hugged each other and released the anxiety of uncertainty during the hour-long loss of communication. Haipin said she had given up trying to keep a short distance from her husband's truck due to many cars going in and out in front of her. It was the few minutes that Yan Yun's entering the service station at a slow speed, alerting her attention on the rental truck. After taking a short break the couple and kids continued their trip south. They stayed overnight at Interstate Inn in the small town of Perry on highway I-35.

After a day of miserable weather through most of the trip, Sunday, November 16th the sky was clear and the couple finally reached their destination, Weatherford, Oklahoma. Several students from Yan Yun's class gathered in front of the new house to welcome their professor's family, and at the same time helped unload the truck.

This was Haipin's 5th family relocation since she came to the United States and her first good impression of a better life in the making. Yan Yun held a good position at the local university. The couple owned a new brick house. She could smell the new paint, the new carpet, and the modern convenience of using a new microwave oven, new refrigerator, new dishwasher and a new washer and dryer.

The Booming Oil/Gas Industry

Another impression was the business booming in the small city with a population of less than 15,000. The big demand of oil and gas at that time had made the oil rich depository soil of this region a place where the treasure hunting businessmen invested their money. Oil well drilling rigs could be seen everywhere, near the city as well as the remote rural area. The oil/gas drilling business brought a booming local economy. The local newspaper had an oil well report. It seemed the number increased every week. Any job seeker would be thinking about getting a job in this oil gas industry.

The energetic workaholic Haipin never thought about being idle at home as a full time housewife. Now her kids were in school: one in pre-school and the other in second grade. It would be better than before for her to work full time outside the home. She did not mind smelling gas at the drilling sites that needed workers. However, no drilling company ever thought of hiring a female employee to work in the open field rigs. She began to think of alternatives. And her busy life in the new environment began.

Job Versatility

Since Haipin had experience in seeking unskilled jobs in her previous employment, she was familiar with the source of the labor market. Upon settling down at the new residence, she contacted the government employment service for help. Haipin received several referrals from the agency. Some jobs were available immediately, while the better paying positions were not. The point of Haipin's being a workaholic was to catch the opportunity in time and work today, not an unrealistic dream of an ideal job that would not be available until in the distant future, or maybe never.

For the first several months, Haipin did not intend to work full time. In fact, she did not have a car that provided transportation to work any distance outside the home.

One day she took a walk around her neighborhood and stopped at the Little Bird Nursing Home. She introduced herself to the manager and told her about her family and being new to the community. The manager welcomed Haipin. They had a warm conversation. After knowing Haipin's plan to find permanent employment, the manager asked her if she would like to work at the nursing home temporarily. The manager said the nursing home always had a vacancy because the working environment (taking care of the elderly, as well as the poor- health people) and low pay could not retain a worker for very long.

It surprised the manager that Haipin accepted the offer and would like to start work the next morning. Thus Haipin returned to work again a couple of weeks after she quit her job at Rockwell International in

Atchison, Kansas. Her crane operator experience at Rockwell was quite different from the current position as being a nurse's aide.

Aware of the necessity of driving a car to work outside home, the couple bought a new 1979 Zephyr station wagon. This would meet Haipin's transportation needs as well as the needs of family outdoor recreation. This was a new milestone for the family, owning a new house and two cars.

On August 20th, 1979, Haipin quit the nurses aide position and filled a vacancy at the Kellwood Company, a maker of bedding items, 15 miles from her home. She began to learn how to operate huge sewing and quilting machines. This job required very little muscle strength, and the production floor was clean with air conditioning, so she could sit all the time at work.

Haipin believed she would be able to do something more challenging at the same time. Going back to college came to her mind. She enrolled in the current fall semester for three college credit hours in accounting at the local university. The class met twice each week at 7 o'clock in the evening.

The energetic woman had filled her available time fully, beginning with getting up and preparing for work at five in the morning, returning home from work at four o'clock, sharing a warm family union with her husband and kids. At 7 p. m. she was in her accounting class or working on class assignments at the accounting lab on evenings she did not have a class. She did not go to bed until midnight. The blue-collar worker, professor's wife, and mother of two school kids seemingly enjoyed the hustle and bustle life more than seeking relaxation time at home.

Haipin had thought of finding a better paying job that was located closer to her home. Apparently the 3M company was her target. She had been invited to the 3M facility for job interviews a couple of times. Each time she was informed to wait for openings at a later time. However, she never gave up her desire to work for the company. Finally, twenty two months later, on September 23, 1981, she started working there in a permanent full time data production position, wearing a white technician robe uniform.

Compared to her previous blue-collar job, this data processing work was the best she had ever held. Haipin worked in a climate-controlled, well-lighted, well-sealed laboratory environment designed to avoid dust that might be falling on the film surfaces of the computer floppy diskettes. Her wage was double, compared to her pay at Kellwood Bedding Company. She did not need to get up early in the morning in order to beat the traffic and it was a 15 mile drive one way.

Haipin did not enjoy the current stable family life for very long. Her husband left his teaching position at the local university and moved to Lawton, working on a Federal grant project at a university there. He was offered only half the salary he made at his previous employment. Since it was a temporary appointment, Haipin and the kids did not move with Yan Yun to Lawton, which was 105 miles one way. To respond to the new situation that her husband would not be able to share family chores, especially taking care of the kids, Haipin discontinued her business classes at the university and did not work over time at 3M company.

Unfortunately, another disappointment followed. Yan Yun was out of work, ending the contract on the Federal funding project at Carmon University due to the discontinuance of the government grant. He worked there only ten months. Since then he became frustrated during an 18-month long unemployment period.

"School Lunch Doesn't Seem That Tasty"

As Yan Yun was still home without the possibility of returning to work in sight, Haipn fell into a similar situation. She lost her job on August 1st, 1982. It was a shock to the 'workaholic' woman. Her employer, due to the workforce reduction plan laid her off. She was two months short in seniority to survive the layoff. This was the local 3M unit's first time to lay off employees in its history. Though the company promised, if business turned profit again, to recall her, based on seniority order, Haipin believed that she probably would not have such a miracle.

Financially, this was the worst time for the family of four: from a two paycheck income to one, and then to nothing. The house mortgage payment, the home insurance, the health care, the utility bills, the food, and the kids' school lunches could not stop because of unemployment. Haipin decided to go to work as an on-call nurse's aide at Little Bird Nursing Home. Though it was better than no income, it helped Haipin maintain a normal, active life.

A couple of months passed without a prospective employment opportunity, The couple tried to look for some way of cutting expenses. Since the couple was unemployed, their kids were qualified for free lunch at schools. Haipin supported her husband's decision to suspend buying lunch tickets for their daughter, a first grader, and son, a 4th grader.

To suspend buying school lunch tickets was a decision that the couple made reluctantly. Both Yan Yun and Haipin were uncomfortable when they received a note of approval form from the school district. Though it was a temporary emergency alternative, the couple regretted that they did act on the matter. They believed it was the parents' responsibility to provide support, not that of other taxpayers.

Haipin wondered how her kids felt about the free lunch. Usually the kids enjoyed the variety of the lunch menu every weekday. They never complained about the taste, and Ray, the oldest, would tell his mother what his favorite food was. Since he was on a free lunch program, Ray, had kept silent on the school lunch activity. One day he indicated to his mother that he was a little uncomfortable about joining the free lunch group. He said the "**lunch seems not that tasty.**"

Ray's feelings touched Haipin's heart. She considered canceling the free lunch request, even though there was no prospect in sight of returning to full time employment, for either her husband or herself. Currently her son had been on the free lunch program for one month. She set one month as her goal of taking her son out of the government aid program.

It seemed a miracle that Haipin's wish came true. On October 13th, 1982, her husband got a confirmation about his new appointment for an administrative position at a community college in Fort Worth, Texas effective on the first of November. The couple immediately notified the local school district to take their kids off of the free lunch program. Now the family regained their pride of independence and hard work.

Yan Yun's first paycheck was not due until November, a couple of months away. In fact, both Yan Yun and Haipin were still unemployed. The family was not yet free from financial hardship. They still prayed for something that would help them out.

Haipin never knew that a miracle would knock on her door again. After more than seven months of being laid off from work, she was called back to work on March 20th, 1983. The 3M company would pay the same wages she earned before the layoff. Though it was a delayed rescue, it indeed was a much needed income to pay for the relocation cost when they moved to Texas. Yan Yun had already reported to his new position at the community college in Fort Worth, Texas on the first of November, 1982. Haipin and kids would move to the new residence in May, 1983. She was tired of moving around so frequently and wished to settle down in Texas for quite a long time.

NINE

Home in Texas

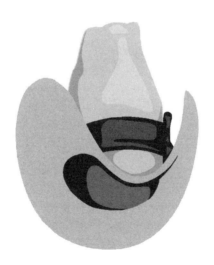

Chapter Nine

Having an opportunity to go back to her old job at 3M's data processing unit at Weatherford, Oklahoma made Haipin very happy. She liked the working environment of data processing. She liked the new house the family owned in the university town. However she had no other choice but to follow her husband's career path of moving around. This time they would move southward to Texas, the Lone Star state. Though Haipin did not know what job opportunity she might have there, she had confidence that she could find a job in the metropolitan Dallas/Fort Worth area. She did wish the family would settle down and provide a stable environment for the kids' growth and allow them to pursue a good education as well.

Haipin and her two kids did not move to Texas until the son and daughter got out of school for the spring semester at the end of May 1983. This was the 6th and the smoothest family moving experience of the couple's relocation operations in the United States.

The couple did not encounter any difficulty selling the five-year old house at their Weatherford, Oklahoma residence. One of Haipin's co-workers at 3M company paid a deposit for purchasing the house several months before she moved out. The couple enjoyed a net gain of $10,000 by selling the house. This amount was a good part of the funding to purchase a new house in Texas.

The growth of the family: husband, wife, 12-year old son, 9-year old daughter, furniture for four rooms, a sedan, and a station wagon was no longer a simple one small car move as it was the first time from Cape Girardeau, Missouri to Norman, Oklahoma in 1970. This time the move involved a fleet of three vehicles. One of the family's friends drove a large U-Haul truck loaded with furniture and large articles. The couple and kids rode in the family cars. They made this one-day moving trip smoothly also.

Spirits Rebound

Haipin looked at this relocation as an important mile-stone of their family life. She and her husband had been struggling to survive for almost two decades since coming to this country. Through her husband's determination and hard work, he had obtained the needed education to have a good chance of winning in the competitive professional job markets. The kids were in school and needed little nanny care. The couple was in the mid-age. Both had suffered unemployment for quite a long time. Haipin wished for no more relocations, no more crises, but being able to enjoy peaceful life and support their kids' well being.

The ever-big family move to Texas took place on Saturday, May 28th, 1983. Despite hot summer weather, every one was in a good mood all the way from Weatheford, Oklahoma to Fort Worth, Texas. Though he was relatively new in this area, seven months exactly, Yan Yun could motivate several local friends to welcome

Haipin and the kids. Friends helped to make the unloading task easier. The kids were busy moving their belongings to their rooms. Haipin could imagine the hard work her husband did involving decisions concerning the new house; from selecting the location, the house plan, the price, and the bank mortgage loan (11.5% interest, a good bargain in 1982). Later she found out the two major criteria of her husband's decision-making on the house. One was the potential of Haipin's employment with Motorola, about one mile away from the house, and the kids' education with Keller school district, a quiet suburban small town in Fort Worth at that time. Probably Yan Yun had yet another unrevealed intention, which was a permanent residence. Haipin had a strong intention of settling down in Texas too.

As a 'workaholic' type woman, Haipin was eagerly preparing to work again in the newly resided community. At the same time she realized that it was also the best time to do things she might not be able to do when she would hold a full time job. Wasn't it time to visit her mother and siblings in Manila? School was not in session until the fall semester began in August. Wasn't it time to take the kids for a short summer vacation overseas?

Haipin and her kids started their vacation in Manila on June 7th and returned home on August 16, 1983. This was a relaxing time that she had dreamed of for a while. Besides visiting her beloved mother and spending time with her son and daughter, it was also a time to revitalize her energy and spirits for meeting the challenge of new jobs ahead.

Upon returning home from the overseas trip, Haipin wasted no time beginning her search for a full time job. Her previous data processing experience with 3M Company led her to focus on an electronic manufacturing job. She sent applications to area businesses with an eye on Motorola's local plant, less than one mile from home.

It was lucky that only Motorola, Haipin's first choice, responded to her inquiry. Two weeks after sending her resume, she, on Wednesday, September 7, 1983, got a call from the company's human resources department for a preliminary job interview. Haipin held the interview, which lasted almost until the evening meal. Motorola confirmed her employment during the interview and she was scheduled to start work on Friday, the 16th of September. Again she was back to working full time.

Haipin successfully completed a certification program for the position as solder during probation period. She was one of the top solders, whose work passed quality control over 99% to 100%. Thus the two-paycheck income family started to build financial stability for the family.

The conditions that might limit Haipin's devotion fully to her job were diminishing as the kids were growing and advancing in academic levels in school.

Her husband's time availability and expertise on kids' education development helped the 'workaholic' woman have even more confidence in her job. She never turned down over time schedule. Whenever she was asked to do a double shift she always willingly accepted.

Haipin's positive attitudes toward the job and maintaining good production standards received incentive rewards. She never missed a single scheduled salary/wages raise, which was between the range of medium and top. She had been honored as employee of the month several times during her tenure with the company.

Changing Lanes

No one could predict things happening beyond one's control. Haipin had ups and downs in her career. She looked at losing a job as an unavoidable thing and tried not to worry too much. Instead, she considered temporary unemployment as a short time break, waiting for a new opportunity with a new beginning. It is just like driving on the highway, in that we can have many opportunities to change lanes.

Motorola's Fort Worth division decided to move the operation, which Haipin was a member, to Florida. Seven hundred employees working on this department were affected. Ironically, in 1990, Haipin was rewarded a 7-year service certificate thanking her for an excellent job well done. However, she was laid off two months before her 8-year anniversary on the job. Her last day with Motorola was July 5th, 1991.

Idling an energetic worker to do only housewife chores was not Haipin's preference. She had been actively searching for a stable position after leaving Motorola. However, she did not have much luck. Haipin thus took a more practical approach toward securing a job. Her new philosophy is

> 'A job is a job. It is better to have a less interesting job than to have an ideal job that might not be available for a while. Time is money. Why wait and lose income.'

Haipin's new strategy at present was to try to find a temporary position. She found that the profit-driven private employment agencies are better places to go for help. The reason is understood. They make profits from a job seeker's paycheck. Haipin worked from one temporary job to another during her unsecured employment time. Do not believe that temporary positions might require fewer qualifications as compared to a full time permanent job. Haipin had been declined a packing position because she failed to lift a 75-bound box.

The 'workaholic' Haipin always had 'work' in mind. In order not to take more working time out for personal leaves while on the paid job, she would best use the jobless period for visiting long missed family and relatives. She took the advantage of not having a job in prospective for a little while during the on and off temporary employment to visit her relatives in the Philippines. Haipin stayed with her mom in Manila for three months in the fall of 1992.

She returned home on the eve of Thanksgiving Day just in time to celebrate the holiday season with her husband, son, and daughter. The warm welcome by her mother, siblings, and friends in Manila during the three-month family union did not change her mind on working outside the home. Neither did Haipin change her mind in sharing financial support for the family, though her husband's college salary could support her as a full time housewife and mother.

Haipin launched a full scale search for employment. She registered with Texas employment centers and local temporary job service for assistance. She also walked into personnel offices of retail stores as well as major manufacturers for openings. She did work various jobs, all of them were temporary in nature.

Until Nokia Mobile Phones (formerly TNC) offered her a full time permanent position on February 10, 1993 Haipin considered claiming the end of her two years uncertainty in searching for a permanent position after leaving Motorola.

As soon as Haipin completed a couple of days orientation on the new job, she could feel the prospects of the company in becoming a major corporation in the cellular phone industry. Working over time had become her routine. The number of additional hours could range from eight to 20 each week. New assembly lines were added in a short interval. A parking lot for the employees continued to be expanded. Later Nokia moved its manufacturing facility to a newly developed large industrial park at Alliance Gateway area in north Fort Worth, Texas to accommodate the company's fast growing needs.

Haipin started her work with Nokia at the company's old production facility at Diplomacy St. in Irving, Texas about 20 miles one way from her home. She worked the second shift from 4 p.m. to midnight. Her over time might be from midnight to early the next morning, noon to midnight, or on Saturday or Sunday. It was not a good shift for most workers. Haipin, however, remained on this shift for five years, showing no sign of being bored or compromise of quality and quantity. She maintained a good record of perfect attendance. Her only regrettable thing was missing her kids most of the day, though her educator husband did a good job in taking care of them.

The 'workaholic' woman could be called a strong and confident 'brave female' too. She drove alone on Highway 10 and Trinity Blvd. to and from work through miles of a less populated area, with few roadside lights, but with a lot of bushes and trees alongside the route. During the night, the traffic was relatively slow and occasionally a police car would patrol there. However, a woman alone traveling this area is vulnerable to robbery or sexual assault. Haipin had never thought of quitting the job.

She did experience a few incidents that bothered her. Once a car followed her at the same speed. It was very strange that the headlights were off and on, then, passed her in front, then, followed her in back on the same lane again. She first thought the driver might be drunk. She tried not to be frightened. Instead, Haipin kept calm and continued on her way home. In an emergency though she could not remember all the do's and don'ts. She had one 'don't' in mind and that was, 'do not get out of the car.' She probably could have had peace of mind, had wireless phones been available at that time. Anyway there are a lot of crazy people on the streets; many of them leaving the bar at night. Haipin could only pray for good luck.

One night on the way home from work, Haipin saw a police patrol car signaling her to stop for questioning. She was not afraid of an officer whose duty is to protect the general public. At the same time Haipin also learned from crime reports in newspapers that frequently criminals could dress and act as real police officers in an attempt to rob a helpless traveler. A lone traveler, especially a woman, such as Haipin, traveling through the quiet wooded area at midnight was an easy target for a criminal attack.

Keeping this conflict in mind, the good versus bad, Haipin chose the good one, believing that she might get help such as changing a flat tire from the police patrol officer. She was no longer in fear that something might be against her. As the patrol officer approached her, it turned out to be a friendly conversation. The officer did not ask for her driver's license, but wanted to know whether she was from a nightclub and if she had been drinking. Then he praised her for being a career minded woman, not afraid of driving home at midnight. Haipin found that it was her driving and signaling that caught the officer's attention.

It was a routine drive from work at 1:20 am on October 10, 1993. Usually the traffic was slow at that time of night. As a caution Haipin had a special alert of possible safety issues while passing through the wooded section of the highway. She saw no other cars or pedestrians nearby. While proceeding to travel across an intersection with a green signal light, a speeding vehicle passed through the red light and hit her 1990 Ford Topez. Both cars were damaged, but still drivable.

Suddenly the driver involved in this accident got out of his car and demanded Haipin pay $500 for his damaged vehicle. To do so, he would not file a claim with her insurance company and he would not call the police. Meanwhile Haipin was aware that it was not an auto accident, but possibly a planned plot. Apparently it was his fault to pass through a red traffic light that caused the accident. Under the confusion and terrifying situation Haipin did not know how to answer the driver's demand. She did not have the money. At that moment, Haipin thought about the worse situation, that her life was in danger.

During conversation with the driver, he suddenly stopped the negotiation and fled the scene with his car. A police patrol car was approaching the intersection. Haipin told the officer about the accident, but under such a frightening situation, she was not able to give the police the make of the vehicle or description of the driver because of the poor visibility under the dim moonlight. Neither did she get the license tag number of the vehicle involved in the accident.

The police did give Haipin an accident report. Meanwhile the officer said they would investigate the case and try to catch the fleeing driver. Haipin was lucky that she did not get hurt. Her car was still functional so she could continue her trip home and return to work the next day. The insurance paid her car repair bill. This accident did alert her of the need for better protection while traveling through this part of the highway at night. Later she did make friends with a co-worker to go home with her taking the same route. The co-worker happened to be a resident of a neighboring community. Haipin felt safer while going home with her friend's car following her. A safety improvement was made a couple of months later. It was a car pool that Haipin and co-workers drove, rotating schedules, taking the airport freeway home. There was not a problem since then.

The 'workaholic' Haipin got another boost of her spirits when Nokia moved its main production to a new facility in Alliance Gate Way Industrial Park in north

Fort Worth in 1995. She reported to the new facility on November 13. The move gave her many advantages. Instead of driving 20 miles one way to work, the new facility was only 10 miles away from her home. Her three years seniority with the company allowed her an option to choose one of the three working shifts. Haipin then could change from night schedule to the first shift in the morning.

In order to meet the fast growing demand of production, the facility operated 24 hours a day, seven days a week with three shifts. Employees might be required to work 12 hours a day in some cases. It was not unusual for Haipin to work consecutive two weeks without taking a day off. The excellent job performance made Haipin a popular worker to be rewarded for over time assignment. Her name remained on the perfect attendance list every time. In 2003 Nokia honored Haipin with a 10 year service certificate. She is still a full time hard working employee with the company today. Haipin is proud of her accomplishment as a blue-collar worker, no less than her previous teaching career in Taiwan. She believes that every job is important to our life and our society. Certainly as a 'workaholic' woman, Haipin would not abandon her hard working nature on jobs that she might be qualified to perform.

It has been a fortunate opportunity that Haipin and her husband have secured full time permanent employment in the Lone Star state, choosing to settle down in the metropolitan Fort Worth area. After years of moving around from one place to another, it was time for the hard working Haipin to enjoy family life in the urban community. The caring of her children's growth, both physically and mentally has been an important part of her daily life.

What ... ? If ...

Like most parents who have school age kids, Haipin had to share responsibility with her husband, providing guidance for their children's education and behavior. When the family settled down in the urban Fort Worth community in 1983, Ray, her son, then, 12, enrolled at a local junior high as a seventh grader, and daughter, Joy, 9, a 4th grader at an elementary school. The kids were getting closer to becoming 'teenagers'.

Haipin was glad to see her children growing into 'teenagers'. They certainly would be more independent. However, it is also true that 'teenagers' are at a restless stage in their life. To discipline kids for violating family rules is a kind of headache for every parent. Haipin and her husband were raised in the Chinese old tradition. To raise a child in the modern American society was really a big challenge for them. The couple had doubts about the 'grounding a kid' practice that is prevalent in American families, as to whether it would be workable for them.

It was logical for Haipin, a former elementary schoolteacher, and her husband, Yan Yun, a university professor and certified high school faculty to work out something on the popular 'ground' rule. The couple totally avoided the use of 'grounding' to punish the kids for their undesirable behavior. Instead, they employed results based thinking of '**What**', and '**If**' for action.

The '**what**' and '**if**' theory works this way. Before an action is taken, parents should think **what** would be the results; that is, the reaction from the child, **if** a given rule is carried out. It is a positive and human understanding approach to the child with love. This disciplinary approach has been developed as an alternative option to the grounding rules that Haipin learned from her co-workers and friends about the headaches of carrying out grounding rules. The worst case was the child's strong negative reaction to parents' grounding rule by going in the opposite direction, such as running away from home. A scary story was once reported in a Chinese language newspaper in the United States. For example, an immigrant family from Taiwan, when returning home from a couple of days vacation found vandalism in their house. Party trash (leftover food) was everywhere: in the living room, bedroom, and bathroom. Graffiti could be seen on the living room wall. More irritating to the parents was the absence of their teenage son, who was asked that during the parents absence, to stay home and not to invite anyone, including his good friends to mess up the house. Though the teenage boy hated the parents' tough rules and had been grounded many times, he never had openly challenged dad and mom's authority.

Could we, as parents, find better solutions than tough ground rules? The answer is yes. Haipin and her husband never introduced a ground rule for Ray and Joy. The couple always gave the kids' room to find a way out, should they do their best effort, but failed in some areas. This had avoided a clash between parents and children.

For example, a slumber party, hanging out with peers of the opposite sex, and dating are common activities of teenagers and they are an adolescent's normal behavior. Though tough-grounding rules might work for some, it could fail for others. Haipin looked closely at her teens behavior on these activities. She would first think about **WHAT** could be the result **IF** she granted her kids permission. Haipin would tell the kids what mom would like to do in this matter if she were a kid. It was a routine practice that Haipin and her husband applied. This was kind of a suggestive gesture instead of a warning of the serious consequences. The confident woman has been a lucky mom. She never had any serious problems handling her teens' behavioral disciplinary problems. And she thus could find more time to devote to the kids' education.

The Applause

Haipin was pleased to notice that the change of the learning environment from a small school to a large urban district did not affect her children's academic ability. This new residency in Fort Worth, Texas was the couple's third relocation since her kids attended public schools in three states: Kansas, Oklahoma and Texas.

For a mom, the children's school activities and honors that frequently made good news for the immigrant family was one of Haipin's unforgettable memories at that stage of life. She had never been so excited over the kids' school accomplishments as one after another continued when her family moved to Fort Worth, Texas. She believes that she simply was a lucky mom.

Both her son and daughter when starting 7th and 4th grade respectively in Keller ISD, Fort Worth, were on the top ten, and later on National Junior High Honor Society.

They kept academic excellence from high school through college. Particularly, Ray, the oldest child. Though a quiet boy at home, he had become a shining star in the academic field in school and a spot light in the local newspaper as well.

Their son's high school junior and senior years had the most academic activities on and off campus. The results were to bring home honors: such as teacher's notes, winning prizes, certificates, and trophies. Co-workers congratulated her for her son's winning of a Motorola scholarship. The news was published on the electronic board in the cafeteria of the company. Haipin's son won the National Merits Scholarship 1989. Anyone could imagine how proud mom was among her colleagues.

Then came another honor for her son. Ray was chosen to represent the school district for a scholarship tour to the nation's capitol. A local corporation, American Airlines, financed this project. The three-day Washington tour was designed for the student to learn how the government works. Haipin, for quite a time wished to take her children to visit Washington, D.C. but never had a chance to do so. This guided learning tour was even better than she could have done alone.

Until now Haipin had envied moms who had kids receiving recognition in sports. Thank God, she had a chance to share similar spirits of honor with her son, just as those moms with their sports hero sons. In 1989, the Texas Association of Secondary School Principals for the first time in history honored 25 students for academic excellence as an All State Academic Team. Her son, Ray, ranked 5th on the team selected from more than 300 school districts statewide.

The immigrant mom never dreamed that she and her husband could be in the spotlight at a high school graduation ceremony. Again, her son's academic attainment gave parents such glory. The Keller High 1989 graduation was held in a large auditorium, the TCU sports coliseum. Parents, grandparents, relatives, and friends of the graduating class filled the seats in the huge coliseum. Haipin did not bother asking friends to take a day off from work for this ceremony, neither her family members overseas could come to share her son's honors. Having the feeling of being just as happy as one of the hundreds of parents of the graduating class,

Haipin and her husband sat amidst a crowded balcony, having excited, but peaceful moments watching their son receive his diploma while passing the podium.

Before awarding the high school diploma, distinguished students in sports, academic subjects, and students in community service were given certificates. In addition, Ray was given a short introduction, honoring his academic accomplishments as top of the top ten. The length and loudness of applause seemed to reflect the extent that the audience recognized the students' achievement.

Then the focus turned to Ray. The announcer on the podium introduced the valedictorian, as he was about to deliver the speech for the graduating class of 1998. At the same time, the spotlight was on his parents. The audience gave Haipin and her husband a loud applause. The immigrant couple received instant fame as they walked from the coliseum. Many people from the crowd extended congratulations to the proud parents by shaking hands and praising their good guidance to their child's success.

Some curious parents wished to find out the immediate academic plan of the valedictorian. As they heard his almost perfect SAT and ACT scores, 20 hours credit AP tests, and the winner of several national and state scholarships as well. Haipin, could not hide her feelings about her son's thoughtfulness of being close to his parents. Ray did not choose Harvard, MIT, Stanford, but the home state flag university, UT-Austin. He was admitted to the honors program of aerospace engineering.

During Ray's first college program years, Haipin never heard things she would not want to hear from campus. Instead she enjoyed receiving good news frequently from Ray's academic accomplishments. Each year he brought home a certificate of recognition of his aerospace engineering scholarship.

Haipin, the immigrant mom, and her husband, shared the spot light at the graduation as the college dean hung a medal on Ray's neck and handed over to him the diploma of Bachelor of Science in Aerospace engineering with the highest honors. Then a loud applause followed. Another honor for her son was that he was the only one among the 31 graduating classes that was rewarded with the certificate of completion of a five-year engineering program in four years.

Children's academic news continued to make Haipin's life exciting. Now it was her young daughter's turn to make good days. In addition to her continuing to maintain excellent academic status in school, Joy had a talent in communications skills. She liked social activity and made friends easily. American democratic society has naturalized the immigrant's second-generation. Joy, with the value of independent thinking, expressed her personal views and respected the views of others.

Children in early ages could touch some sensitive feeling on cultural diversity. One evening during spring semester 1984, Joy shared her experience with her mother. Several of her 4th grade classmates ridiculed her Chinese heritage. She said she did not cry. Instead she was able to defend her culture by arguing,

"I am smart, one of the two straight 'A' students in my class.   My brother is also a straight A student in his class. If the Chinese did not invent firecrackers we would not be able to have fireworks to celebrate the Fourth of July.   Children might not have any new toys [toys in the market at that time were mostly made in Taiwan and Honk Kong.]"

Joy once again demonstrated her talent in argument. She represented junior high kids, speaking against licensing liquor stores in the local community at a public hearing.   Later Haipin was delighted to know that her daughter had taken a position in the school newsletter as contribution writer and editor, as well as from junior high through high school.

As a proud mom, Haipin was pleased to see her daughter developing her talent from high school to college with the subject she was much interested in. Joy earned a Bachelor of Journalism with higher honors from the University of Texas at Austin. Haipin and her husband had another time to share the applause at a graduation ceremony for their other child in 1998.

To Haipin, it seems as if it were yesterday when she flew to the states alone as a young woman, struggling to survive as a student wife in 1968. However, time has passed by long enough to make her and her children's generations flourish into the great American society. Now her children have earned college degrees with higher honors and are starting careers.

In 1998, Ray earned a graduate degree, Master of Science in computer science with highest honors. He is an engineer working in the aerospace and computer industry. Ray and wife Wei Fen, an SMU (Dallas, Texas) law school graduate student, have a lovely family with twin kids, Connor and Amanda.

In a different field of accomplishment Haipin is proud of her daughter's pursuing human service career. Currently Joy works with a non-profit social service organization assuming a directorship position.

Each stage of our life has a mission. For Haipin, the mission of becoming a student wife, the mission of raising children, and the mission of achieving a rewarding career have merged hand-in-hand in the struggle to be a success as an immigrant family. And it has paid off; enjoying a happy life in a warm family.

The Haunting Sea Gull And The Roaring Cow

It is hard to believe that the immigrant couple (Haipin and Yan Yun's) survival expedition trail would follow a historical reverse direction of eastern and south central-ward and landing in the big cowboy country - Texas.

Having been a resident for decades in the Big State, Haipin watched her children grow during the critical, important part of their life: from teenage to adult, from college education to securing prospering careers.

Certainly Haipin never overlooks the understanding of a well-educated husband that contributes a warm and peaceful family environment: more supportive, less complaining, more respectable, less arrogant, getting mutual consensus, but less divisive to raise the children.

The employment stability over two decades in the community of Fort Worth, Texas has made Haipin feel welcome, as well as comfortable to proudly claim a home. Motorola offered her a full time permanent position while moving to this neighborhood as a new resident. Haipin remained as a top productive hard working employee, devoting her time and energy to this corporation for almost eight years until the company's reorganization.

Her excellent productivity with a valuable sense of responsibility, dependability, and perfect attendance has been recognized by the continuous employment with Nokia Mobile Phone (USA) since 1993 after leaving Motorola.

Haipin has never sought for a supervisory position with her college education and excellent blue-collar assembly line job performance. She rather enjoys personal satisfaction in doing what she likes to do and doing it well. This way would eliminate the frustration and disappointment with someone who could not do a good job under her supervision. **A rewarding job, as she describes, 'is a job you like and you have the chance to do it right, and then comes the feeling of accomplishment.'**

As she looks back at her many accomplishments in life, Haipin enjoys living comfortably with her family in her adopted home town, the cowboy country of Fort Worth in the Lone Star state. She never lived in a place for two consecutive decades except her birthplace of Manila, the capital city of the Philippines. As a spoiled child of successful business parents, Haipin would like to visit the seashore with her classmates, watching the sea gulls soar over the sky, wishing to have a good career and happy life in the future. It turns out that her prosperity has been a good life in the United States. Through hard work, her American dream has come true. The soaring sea gull still haunts her in her childhood mind, now the roaring cows become the scenic countryside as she drives outside the city. This is the story of Haipin, through a long journey to reach an American dream goal, having been a school teacher, a student wife, a caring mother, a housewife, a workaholic blue-collar worker, a devoted happy career woman, an immigrant, and a proud American citizen.

(Author's note: the author completed this writing in October 2004 in cerebrating his 40th anniversary with Haipin)

Other titles by the author

Other Titles by the Author

The following books are available online at major online booksellers in the United States, or email at w007745@airmail.net *for more information.*

The Golden Lotus: the life of a bound-feet peasant mother in the Chinese Cultural Revolution
© 2004 ISBN: 0-9675988-3-4 Library of Congress Catalog Card Number: 2004092609, paperback, 5.5 x 8.5   140p. $7.95

It is the true story of a Chinese peasant mother, Pan Chin, caught in the turmoil of China in the mid-20th century. Pan Chin lived a miserable life, crippled by her bound feet and trapped in an unhappy marriage. Living in abject poverty, she endured separation form her two sons, the tragic death of her only daughter, and political persecution during the Cultural Revolution.

My God, It Missed Me!: A young soldier's accounts of the war-torn China 40-50's
© *2002* Library of Congress Catalog Card Number 2002-190002. ISBN 0-9675988-2-6, paperback, 5.5 x 8.5, 164p. $11.95

On July 7, 1937, Japan attacked China, starting the eight-year Sino-Japanese War within World War II. After Japan's surrender to the Allies in 1945, China soon plunged into civil war between the Nationalist forces of Chiang Kai-Shek and the Communist forces of Mao Tse-Tung. The death and destruction caused by these successive wars in China was widespread and enormous. In this book, the author describes his childhood life in a remote mountain village in China, his early education, his drafting into the army during the civil war, and his battle-filled nightmares. Upon one harrowing occasion, a bullet missed him by a mere foot, striking and killing a nearby soldier.

Although World War II and the Chinese Civil War occurred a half-century ago, the effects of those wars still are present in China and Taiwan today. This book details the suffering of the people of China during that tumultuous period in time, and describes a young soldier's fight for survival in those war-torn years. This book is on Bowker's bookwire recommended lists, on war and terrorism on September, 2003.

Where Can I Find It? A Source Handbook for New Immigrants.
© 2000.   ISBN 0-9675988-1-8.   Library of Congress Catalog Card Number 00 093201. Softback, 5 1/2x8 1/2, 200 pages, $9.95.

A handy guide to basic information designed for new immigrants. *Where Can I Find It?* is a unique reference for anyone living in the United States. This book not only provides an introductory look at topics like citizenship, education, employment, but also covers information on licensing, residential life, emergencies, money matters, health, insurance, legal help, traveling, transportation, taxes, public welfare, consumer information, recreation, creative ideas and surfing the Internet. In addition, useful data such as naturalization requirements, INS service centers, major holidays, location and average of temperature of state capitals, postal rates, telephone country codes, etc., are given in the book's appendix. *Where Can I Find It?* is a good source for information for immigrants, those interested in moving to the U.S., and anyone curious about life in the U.S.

Education & Career: An Immigrant's Journey in the Promise Land with Survival Tips.

© 1999.   ISBN 0-9675988-0-X.   Library of Congress Catalog Card Number 99-096346.   Softback, 5 1/2 x 8 1/2, 165 pages, $**7.95**

Although this book is written for the immigrants, any audience who is interested in pursuing education and finding employment would find that the survival tips and authors experiences are helpful. Part one of the book introduces American education systems, academic programs, and the author's experience in earning college degrees. Part two discusses job sources, securing employment, career advancement, and the author's experience in finding, keeping, and securing a job. There are helpful survival tips.

Forthcoming books

The Rough Journey, A Wartime Romance
ISBN 0-9675988-4-2 (Publication date: not set)

This fictional tale relates the adventures of Zhi Hao, a teenage country boy, and Mei Dai, a teenage city girl, struggling to gain an education amid the chaos of the final stages of World War II in China. Air raid sirens become a constant companion to Zhi Hao and his classmates, interrupting their lessons frequently and making them run to the air raid shelter as part of their daily routine. In the 1950's both of them fought the Chinese Civil War. But a chance encounter between Zhi Hao and the beautiful Mei Dai soon blossoms into romance. Can their newfound love survive the Chinese Civil War?